boiling fast while it is melt...
...le is lost waste, & the je...
...ave a brighter appeara...

...No... ...berry je...
Put some st... ...es in...
earthen pan... ...g... th...
well with a new woo...
spoon; mix some f...u...
sugar with the fruit &...
them infuse for an ho...
that the sugar may d...
out all the juice)"; nex...
in a little water. If th...
strawberries are very...
squeeze the juice of 2...
to restore the acid taste...
strawberries, for such p...
...ations as are too sweet...
...sipid. Put all this in...
bag that is nearly new, t...
the juice may be strai...
clear & limpid, mix so...

Nelly Custis Lewis's

Housekeeping Book

Nelly Custis Lewis's Housekeeping Book

Edited with an introduction
by
Patricia Brady Schmit

Mount Vernon Ladies' Association

Published by
The Historic New Orleans Collection
New Orleans, Louisiana
1982

For my father and mother

Title page:
Silhouette of Nelly Custis Lewis, by Charles Peale Polk, c. 1810.
Courtesy Henry Ford Museum, The Edison Institute.

Following Contents:
Portrait of Nelly Custis Lewis by John Trumbull, c. 1815, after
Gilbert Stuart, c. 1800. Courtesy Woodlawn Plantation.

International Standard Book Number: 0-917860-09-8
Library of Congress Catalog Card Number: 82-81038
The Historic New Orleans Collection, New Orleans 70130
© 1982 by The Historic New Orleans Collection
Third Printing, 1992. 2,000 copies.
Printed in the United States of America

Preface

The Butler family papers are among the largest and most significant holdings in the manuscripts division at the Historic New Orleans Collection. With over two thousand items, spanning nearly two hundred years, the papers are a rich source for the study of American history. A selection of these letters are presently being edited for publication.

The housekeeping book of Nelly Custis Lewis is found among the Butler papers because Mrs. Lewis's son-in-law was Edward George Washington Butler. Although the housekeeping book has an intrinsic historic interest and charm, it clearly does not fit within the bounds of the Butler publication project. The decision was made to prepare the manuscript for separate publication, including a biographical essay on Nelly Custis Lewis, because of its reflection of nineteenth-century daily life.

It soon became clear that the recipes in the book would not be fully intelligible to the average modern reader without a good deal of explanatory material on nineteenth-century cooking, medical, and housekeeping practices; yet it was felt that many readers would prefer to use a book of recipes uncluttered with editorial apparatus. The housekeeping book, then, is presented as written without explanatory notes or any reorganization of recipes. An extensive introduction and glossary cover all the recipes, placing them in their historical setting and providing full information on purposes and techniques.

Stanton Frazar, Director

Acknowledgments

Many people contributed to the research and production of this book. Mr. and Mrs. Richard C. Plater, Jr., in addition to their original donation of the manuscript, have been unfailingly supportive of the project. Margaret Davis, program assistant at Woodlawn Plantation, has been a mine of information. She, George Smith, administrator, and Susan Smith, assistant to the administrator, upheld the best tradition of Virginia hospitality when I visited Woodlawn.

Daphne Derven, staff archeologist, United States Corps of Engineers, served as consultant on nineteenth-century cookery; she generously shared her enormous knowledge of the subject, clearing up difficult points and suggesting research sources. For assistance in various areas of research I am very much indebted to Alan Burkett, associate professor of chemistry, Dillard University; Sue Woodward, manuscripts cataloguer, Tulane University library; Ellen McCallister, librarian, Mount Vernon; and E. Lee Shepard, acting editor, Virginia Historical Society.

For their help in securing illustrations, I am most grateful to Timothy Chester, associate curator, Louisiana State Museum; Jan Bradford, curator, Hermann-Grima Historic House; Carol Nelson, director, Magnolia Mound Plantation; Walter E. Simmons, II, curator, Henry Ford Museum; and H. Parrot Bacot, director, Anglo-American Art Museum.

The entire staff of the Historic New Orleans Collection has given generously of both time and knowledge. Rosanne McCaffrey, curator; Florence Jumonville, librarian; Catherine Kahn, archival assistant; and Robert Brantley, special projects researcher; have come to my assistance time and again. Susan Cole, curator of manuscripts, and Alfred Lemmon, archival researcher, were indispensable to the completion of the project.

I am grateful to Stanton Frazar, director of the Historic New Orleans Collection, and the entire board of directors for encouraging me in a project that has been so enjoyable. Mary Louise Christovich read and edited the manuscript, contributing many helpful suggestions and saving me from some embarrassing mistakes.

I want to thank most of all my children, Colin and Elizabeth, for their support through constant disruptions and their assistance as food critics for many of the recipes.

Contents

Introduction

Martha Dandridge m.(1)1749 Daniel Parke Custis
b.1731, d.1802   b.1711, d.1757
m.(2)1759
George Washington
b.1732, d.1799

John Parke   Martha Parke
b.1754, d.1781   b.1755, d.1773
m.(1)1774
Eleanor Calvert m.(2)1783 Dr.David Stuart
b.1758, d.1811
numerous children

Elizabeth Parke
b.1776, d.1832

Martha Parke
b.1777, d.1854

ELEANOR PARKE (NELLY)
b.1779, d.1852
m.1799
Lawrence Lewis
b.1767, d.1847

George Washington Parke
b.1781, d.1857

Frances Parke
b.1799, d.1875
m.1826
Edward G.W. Butler
b.1800, d.1888
2 sons, 2 daughters

Martha Betty
b.1801, d.1802

Lawrence Fielding
b.1802, d.1802

Lorenzo
b.1803, d.1847
m.1827
Esther Maria Coxe
b.?, d.1885
6 sons

Eleanor Agnes Freire
b.1805, d.1820

Fielding Augustine
b.1807, d.1809

George Washington Custis
b.1810, d.1811

Mary Eliza Angela
b.1813, d.1839
m.1835
Charles Conrad
b.1804, d.1878
1 daughter, 2 sons

Introduction

The housekeeping book presented in this volume is a hand-written collection of recipes and remedies kept by Eleanor Parke Custis Lewis (1779-1852), George Washington's adopted daughter. It was preserved among the papers of the Butler family, planters and businessmen prominent in Louisiana history. Although Nelly, as she was called, was a Virginian, her eldest daughter spent most of her life on a Louisiana sugar plantation with her husband, Edward Butler. The manuscript was passed down through the Butler family until it was presented to the Historic New Orleans Collection. The book touches on many aspects of nineteenth-century social history, telling a great deal about the life and responsibilities of a southern lady, mistress of a great plantation.

Eleanor Parke Custis Lewis was one of the most accomplished American women of her day. Better educated than most men, she had a high degree of intellectual curiosity, and she continued educating herself throughout her long lifetime. Through reading from her extensive personal library and through acquaintance with the leading men of the time, she kept abreast of current political and public affairs. Studying French as a young girl, she was very interested in languages; even as a middle-aged woman, she hired a tutor to teach her Spanish. Beautiful and charming, she was also very talented musically and artistically. Her harpsichord playing highlighted many social evenings, and her fancy needlework and paintings decorated her home and those of her many friends and relatives.

Yet, her role in life was predetermined by her being a woman of the Virginia planter class. The only acceptable field of activity for her was marriage and the management of a household and family. Marrying early, giving birth to a large number of children, managing a large household efficiently and graciously was her destined *metiér* in nineteenth-century America. Her other attainments were merely graceful decorations for her true function as housewife. The housekeeping book, then, is a true reflection of her major life employment, the measure of a woman's life.

Nelly was Martha Washington's granddaughter by her first marriage to Daniel Parke Custis. The couple had two children who survived childhood, John Parke Custis (Jacky) and Martha Parke Custis (Patsy). Widowed early, Martha Custis married George Washington in 1759. Despite their love for children, the Washingtons remained childless, and George Washington treated the Custis children as his own. However, the Washingtons were left alone with the death of Patsy in 1773 and Jacky's early marriage. Jacky was a wild, attractive young man who proposed marriage, without Washington's permission, to sixteen-year-old Eleanor Calvert, a descendant of Lord Baltimore. Both sets of parents eventually consented to the match, and in 1774 the young couple married.

Within the next seven years Jacky and Eleanor Custis had four children—Elizabeth Parke, Martha Parke, Eleanor Parke, and George Washington Parke Custis. Nelly, born in 1779, was sent to Mount Vernon to be nursed by the wife of Washington's overseer because her mother was extremely ill following her birth; she remained a semipermanent resident, often joined by her mother and older sisters. These were the years of the American Revolution, so George Washington and Jacky Custis were in the field, seldom joining the women and children at home. Born in 1781, Washington Custis was also sent to Mount Vernon to be cared for. Only a few months after his son's birth, and just as the war was drawing to a close, Jacky Custis died of camp fever.

The Washingtons decided to adopt the two younger Custis children, Nelly and Washington, who had already spent most of their lives at Mount Vernon. With their mother's permission, the children continued to live with the Washingtons. Although no formal adoption papers were signed, they were considered to be the Washingtons' children and were treated differently from the other Custis grandchildren in their education, financial support, marriage settlements, and inheritance. Their mother married Dr. David Stuart in 1783 and moved with her older daughters to Hope Park, a plantation some twenty miles from Mount Vernon; the Stuarts subsequently had a number of other children. There was no estrangement between the families; the Stuarts and the older Custis girls visited Mount Vernon frequently, and Nelly and Washington Custis often passed weeks with their mother at her new home.

Nelly's childhood at Mount Vernon was happy, but very restricted. The only imaginable future for a girl was as wife and mistress of a household; a little girl was expected to begin the lessons of southern ladyhood early. Nelly spent hours with her grandmother, learning by example to manage servants, to greet and to entertain guests, to ensure a proper food supply, to serve the appropriate food and drink on a variety of occasions, to converse graciously, to dress attractively, and to behave with charm and decorum. She was not allowed to enjoy the active outdoor life of her brother. She had to be careful to protect her white skin from the sun with hats, parasols, and gloves, because a fair complexion was one of the most important attributes of beauty for a southern lady. Outdoor play would have been difficult in any case since Nelly, like other girls, dressed like a miniature woman. She wore thread stays, tightly laced to produce the admired small waist, and elaborate dresses of brocade and silk with lace ruffles at the sleeve and neck and a lace cap and fichu.

Girls were expected to acquire a certain number of "accomplishments." They were to sing, to paint, to play one or more musical instruments, and to master plain sewing and decorative needlework. In fact, Nelly was extremely talented in all these areas, and the daily lessons helped her to acquire skills which she enjoyed throughout her life. Naturally, a child did not find all the practice pleasant. Martha Washington was extremely strict with Nelly, particularly about her music lessons. Nelly thought their grandmother spoiled her little brother, resenting his freedom. Washington Custis played and ran while Nelly practiced the harpsichord for hours at a time, alternately playing and crying, crying and playing.

Moral and religious training were also essential to the formation of Nelly's character. Mrs. Washington inculcated the strict moral code that Nelly was to follow throughout her life. She was a very active and devout Episcopalian. Most Sundays the Washingtons attended church service, and Bible reading and prayers were a feature of the evening at Mount Vernon.

For many southern girls, a little basic reading, writing, and figuring would have completed an adequate education. However, George Washington believed it essential that Nelly, as well as her brother, should receive a very good education. He insisted that she write well, legibly and grammatically, and express herself elegantly. He wanted Nelly to be knowledgeable about history and politics, and to have some ability in foreign languages, as well as the more usual feminine accomplishments. From an early age the Custis children had a resident tutor at Mount Vernon, who usually doubled as Washington's secretary. The most important of these tutors was Tobias Lear, a Harvard graduate who had studied in Europe, and who was able to give the children an excellent educational foundation.

When Washington was elected President in 1789, Nelly's life changed dramatically. In New York, the first capital, Nelly was enrolled in a fashionable girls' school where she studied reading, English, grammar, plain sewing and embroidery, geography, painting, music, dancing, and French. She was also privately tutored in music and painting by talented artists. The President took Mrs. Washington and the children for a coach ride every Saturday and to church on Sunday. They also joined expeditions to local beauty spots in company with the John Adams family and other high government officials.

When the capital moved to Philadelphia in December 1790, the eleven-year-old Nelly for the first time became part of a close-knit band of friends; these girls remained her friends for the rest of her life. Her most intimate friend was Elizabeth Bordley, with whom she maintained a lifelong correspondence, the source of a good deal of biographical information. Although the Washingtons worried a little about the girls' silliness, chattering, and giggling, Nelly also continued to work hard at her education—studying art, foreign languages, and music. As her skill grew, she began to play the harpsichord for company. As she became older, Nelly was drawn into the social whirl of the nation's temporary capital. She delighted in society and loved nothing more than teas, drives, parties, and light flirtations with eligible young men. Being the adopted daughter of the President would have distinguished her in any company, but Nelly herself had all the attributes to attract admiration. A beautiful brown-eyed brunette, with a lively, teasing air, fond of dancing and music, she was constantly sought after. Apparently none of the young men she encountered made a very serious impression on her, though some of them seem to have been considerably smitten. Nelly tended to take a mildly derisive attitude toward her admirers.

Although she was often bored by official activities and annoyed by the manners of some congressmen, Nelly reveled in the active social life of Philadelphia and the status of being a member of the presidential family. Two long visits to Virginia—to Hope Park in 1795 and to Mount Vernon in 1796—bored her dreadfully. She could hardly bear to talk of Washington's retirement. At the inauguration of President Adams in 1797, she had trouble controlling herself, trembling with the unhappiness she felt. On the trip back to Virginia, the despondent Nelly made a troublesome passenger in the Washingtons' overloaded coach. Besides mounds of luggage, she brought home with her a parrot and a pet dog.

Mount Vernon could not match the excitement of Philadelphia, for whose joys Nelly continued to yearn throughout her life, but it certainly provided a lively social life once the family settled in. Besides the family, the permanent residents at this time included Lafayette's son, who was Washington's namesake, and his tutor, because the marquis had been imprisoned on account of his part in the French Revolution. Mount Vernon was convenient to Alexan-

Pastel of Nelly Custis Lewis, attributed to James Sharples, c. 1799(?). Courtesy Woodlawn Plantation, a Property of the National Trust for Historic Preservation.

dria, Georgetown, and the swiftly growing capital city, then known as Federal or Washington City, so that a constant stream of visitors came to the plantation. The older Custis girls, the Stuarts, and other relatives spent weeks at a time at Mount Vernon. Any visitor to Virginia who could make the shadow of a claim to Washington's acquaintance or with the slightest excuse for an introduction made the pilgrimage to Mount Vernon to meet Washington, often staying for several days.

In fact, Washington found himself increasingly annoyed by the lack of privacy in his home, complaining that Mount Vernon had begun to resemble "a well-frequented tavern" in which he and Mrs. Washington could never dine alone together. The generous Virginia code of hospitality demanded that guests be housed, fed, and entertained with style; for a Virginia planter to be inhospitable was to lose status. Washington, however, found that the almost perpetual presence of guests seriously interfered with his plans and regular habits. He then hit on the expedient of inviting one of his nephews, Lawrence Lewis, the son of his sister, Betty, to serve as deputy host. Each evening Lawrence was to be in charge of entertaining whatever guests were present, while Washington, as was his habit unless the company was particularly distinguished, retired early to bed or to his study to work. He was also to help Washington for an hour or so a day to complete and record some of his papers which he had not been able to complete before leaving Philadelphia.

Lawrence Lewis was a thirty-one-year old childless widower. Although he held the title of major from two brief forays into the army, he had not made the military his career. Enjoying a small independent income, he had not devoted himself with concentration to any occupation. He was thus free to move to Mount Vernon in August, 1797, to help his uncle and to make himself generally useful. He was not paid for his services, but came to take over more and more of the Washingtons' affairs, helping them in many ways.

At first, the idea of making a match between Lawrence and Nelly seemed farfetched. The difference in age was not so important as the difference in dispositions. Nelly was lively, energetic, animated, full of fun and jokes, fond of travel, parties, and society. Even as a young man, Lawrence was grave and serious, dignified and of a retiring disposition. Nelly was generally admired by male visitors, who always commented on her beauty and charm, but she had not yet apparently been herself struck. A brief flirtation with Charles Carroll, handsome and of a distinguished family, involving a number of dances at a ball and a visit by young Carroll to Mount Vernon, had not resulted in a proposal.

Nelly had known Lawrence since childhood, but she now came to know him better and to admire his virtues. She described herself to her friend, Elizabeth Bordley, as being "surprised by cupid." Apparently being members of the same household enabled the couple to improve their acquaintance and to fall in love. Although a romantic attachment was desirable, it was by no means considered necessary for a respectable and happy marriage. Marriage was a family and financial matter, as well as a personal one. Parents expected to have a great deal to say about the choice of a mate. Husbands and wives were expected to come from the same social circle and to be able financially to maintain an appropriate standard of living.

By Virginia standards it was well past time for Nelly to settle down. Girls were expected to marry in their teens, and a girl who reached twenty without marrying was a scorned and pitied old maid. Nelly was no doubt ready to give up her role as a Virginia belle since marriage was considered the only proper state intended by God for human beings.

Nelly spent the Christmas holidays of 1798 with her mother and family at Hope Park. She probably took that opportunity to discuss Lawrence's proposal with her mother because on her return to Mount Vernon in January 1799, she and Lawrence surprised the Washingtons with the news of their engagement and plans for an early marriage.

Although Washington was surprised, he was extremely pleased with their plans. From his point of view, Nelly's marriage to Lawrence had a great deal to recommend it. He may have thought that Nelly's vivaciousness would be better tempered by a serious husband. Nelly could expect to be a considerable heiress and, according to the thinking of the time, needed a husband to manage her land and money. It also eased testamentary problems for Washington, since more of his property would be retained within the Washington family with Nelly's marriage to his nephew. The young couple's plan to continue living at Mount Vernon was also appreciated, because Mrs. Washington would not lose her granddaughter's companionship. Washington went to Alexandria to have himself declared Nelly's official guardian and to arrange for a license for their early marriage.

The wedding took place February 22, Washington's birthday. Virginia weddings of that period seldom took place in church, nor did the bridal couple leave immediately on a honeymoon. Instead the wedding was held at the bride's home with a large house-party of friends and relatives who remained for an extended period of parties. Nelly's mother and stepfather and sisters and brothers-in-law came to stay at Mount Vernon some days before the wedding. February 22 dawned clear and very cold; the minister and Nelly's uncle arrived to partake of a large dinner, and Nelly and Lawrence were married at dusk. They remained as part of a family houseparty for two weeks and then began a series of visits. They visited her sister in Georgetown and her mother, and then made a prolonged round of visits to Lawrence's relatives. In late summer they stayed at one of the popular, though primitive, mineral springs resorts in inland Virginia.

In the fall they returned to Mount Vernon permanently because Nelly was expecting their first child. Apparently Washington was feeling some justifiable anxiety about Lawrence's ambition, because he put pressure on the young man to make definite plans for their future. Washington informed Lawrence of the exact nature of the inheritance that Nelly could expect from him. He planned to take some two thousand acres from Mount Vernon for her, including a mill and distillery of some value. Although he wanted the young couple to reside at Mount Vernon, he suggested that they should begin building a house on their property and making improvements. Washington, himself so hardworking, was worried about Lawrence's apparent indolence. He suggested that Lawrence should begin farming the land as a regular occupation. Washington wrote to Lawrence that idleness, even unaccompanied by dissolute habits, was disreputable in itself. At Washington's urging, Lawrence did begin to take up the affairs of the land, but he had no real interest in farming.

After a week's labor, Nelly gave birth to a healthy baby girl, Frances Parke Lewis, on November 27, 1799. She was attended by a doctor and midwife, and her mother and sisters also came to stay. Very weak and unable to walk, Nelly was confined to her bed for nearly a month, and during that month her life was completely changed. The guests left, and Lawrence Lewis and Washington Custis also left on a business trip despite a spell of unusually severe weather. Although the weather was frightfully cold, George Washington insisted on overseeing farming activities and, in doing so, contracted a cold and sore throat. On the night of December 13, he woke with a severe inflammation of the throat. Doctors were called the next morning, but despite, or perhaps partially because of, the most heroic treatments, Washington died the evening of December 14. During that terrible period Nelly was too sick to come downstairs to say goodbye to her adopted father or to support her grandmother. As Washington died, Nelly and her baby cried helplessly upstairs.

Life at Mount Vernon was never the same thereafter. Washington had been the center of life at Mount Vernon; the force and dynamism of his personality had held everything together. Martha Washington was a broken woman, plagued by ill health and sorrow through the rest of her life. When Nelly recovered sufficiently to leave her bed, she joined the family in deep mourning, helping her grandmother answer the hundreds of letters of condolence they received.

In early 1800, the Lewises chose the site for their proposed home, which was to be known as Woodlawn. They had selected Dr. William Thornton, a physician and architect much admired by Washington, to design their house. That summer Dr. Thornton presented them with the plans for an elegant red brick Georgian building, with a central two-story block flanked by one and one-half story cottages, connected to the main house by hyphens. The plans were approved, and work was begun on one of the side cottages.

Woodlawn Plantation. Courtesy Woodlawn Plantation, a Property of the National Trust for Historic Preservation.

The triumph of Thomas Jefferson and the Republican party in 1800 was very difficult for the residents of Mount Vernon to accept. Nelly was particularly bitter over what she saw as a repudiation of Washington and his principles. She continued to have a hostile attitude toward most of the presidents of her lifetime, although she sometimes visited the White House. She simply felt that no one could live up to the standard set by Washington.

Nelly gave birth to another daughter in the summer of 1801, and Mrs. Washington delighted in her two little great-granddaughters. By early 1802, one wing of Woodlawn was nearly complete and ready for occupation, although the central mansion was not finished. But a very hard blow fell when Martha Washington died in May, 1802. Nelly found it almost impossible to recover from her grandmother's death. From birth she had always lived with Martha Washington and considered her her dearest friend and wisest counselor. Even though she had married and had children, she continued to live at Mount Vernon as her grandmother's child.

For the first time she had to face an independent life.

During Mrs. Washington's illness, Nelly's eldest daughter was extremely ill and needed careful nursing. Although she recovered, the younger daughter died within a month of Mrs. Washington's death. To make matters worse, the Lewises were forced to leave Mount Vernon. By the terms of Washington's will, Mrs. Washington enjoyed a life tenancy, but the estate was left to another nephew. Martha Washington's death meant that the Lewises had to leave, and their new home was incomplete and unfurnished. Because Nelly was far along in another pregnancy, they went to stay with Lawrence's sister Betty Carter, where Nelly gave birth to a son who very shortly died.

Thus, the move to Woodlawn was a very melancholy one, preceded as it was by three deaths and the loss of Nelly's long-time home. The early days there were not happy, as Nelly suffered a serious case of the measles, followed by a decline, that is, depression, from which it seemed that she might not recover.

Gradually, however, life at Woodlawn moved from tragedy to a more normal tempo. The eldest daughter, Parke, was a great comfort to both the Lewises. Two healthy children were born, Lorenzo in 1803, and Agnes in 1805. Sometime during this period the house was completed and was furnished with Mrs. Washington's heirlooms, as well as new furniture. During the subsequent years two more sons were born, who died before reaching their second birthdays, and a daughter, Angela, was born in 1813. Although naturally the parents mourned, the death rate for children under five was so high that every family expected to experience the pain of lost children.

The early education of the children was Nelly's task; fortunately she was well prepared to undertake it because of the excellence of her own education. She gave all her children the fundamentals of learning and also prepared the girls in their appointed tasks—housekeeping, cooking, sewing, and drawing. All the family were musical. Nelly played the harpsichord and Lawrence, the violin. The children learned to play at least one instrument. Part of the evening's entertainment, whether or not the family had guests, was a session of family music. For more advanced education, however, it was considered advantageous for children to go away to school. Both Parke and Lorenzo went to school in Philadelphia. But when Agnes was sent to school, a further tragedy occurred. She became ill, and her mother arrived in Philadelphia just in time to care for her in her last days and to prepare her body for burial. Nelly was inclined to be overprotective and fussy about her children's health, but one must realize that she had prepared the bodies of five of her children for burial.

Daily life at Woodlawn during the more than thirty years that the Lewises were permanently in residence took on a calm rhythm related to the agricultural seasons. The role of mistress of a large plantation was comparable to that of executive director of a large enterprise. Although elegant furniture, clothing, and imported foods were purchased, most of the items used at Woodlawn were produced there. Nelly was in charge of a large household staff of slaves, directing their labors, looking after their health, and seeing to their food, clothing, and housing.

The house was expected to be elegantly furnished and well kept with homemade products. Nelly had to be ready to furnish beds for any number of unexpected guests because of the Virginia notion of hospitality. Old friends and acquaintances of George Washington often made it a point to visit Woodlawn when in the capital, as did Lafayette on his triumphal procession through the United States in 1825.

Above all, Nelly had to oversee the food supply for the household, making sure that Woodlawn was continually provided with an abundance of varied and healthful foods. Every day she had to see that an immense and elegant dinner was placed on the table for the family and an unlimited number of guests.

Because of her grandmother's training, Nelly was an able and organized housekeeper. Guests at Woodlawn always commented on the beauty of the house and grounds, the elegance and bounty of the meals, and the charm of the family.

By the mid-1820s, Parke was an old maid by the standards of the day, having reached twenty-four without receiving a serious offer of marriage. Nelly, however, seemed happy to keep her eldest daughter with her to help entertain guests, to teach Angela to play the harpsichord, and to be her companion in painting, walking, and playing music. However, a suitor appeared when Lt. Edward George Washington Butler of the U.S. Army, son of a Revolutionary War hero and a former ward of Andrew Jackson, visited Woodlawn. Butler was an exceptionally handsome young man from a distinguished family in reduced circumstances; since his graduation from West Point, he had attempted to make his way in the world through a military career. He was aide-de-camp to Gen. Edmund Pendleton Gaines, one of the two ranking generals in the U.S. Army. At first Nelly was quite impressed with this young officer, who was equally impressed with Woodlawn and the family living there. But when it became apparent that he was seriously courting Parke, Nelly began to find previously unobserved flaws in his character, intelligence, and tone of mind. Parke was "delicate" in the style of the times, given to headaches, pallor, indigestion, faintness, and lassitude. Her mother believed that she could never survive the traumas of military life and separation from her family.

Despite her mother's objections, however, Parke was quietly determined to marry her handsome young suitor. Nelly finally resigned herself to the inevitable and, after some postponements, arranged a very elaborate wedding in April 1826. The young couple joined Gen. Gaines in Cincinnati, at the headquarters of the western command; Parke, despite her mother's fears, began to thrive, gaining weight, color, and energy. Nevertheless, her mother continued to fret about her daughter's health, to miss her, and to blame her husband for ruining her life. Although in the early years Butler attempted to maintain cordial relations with his mother-in-law, she retained a critical attitude, and the relationship worsened with time.

Nelly was much happier with the marriage of her son, Lorenzo, the following year, to Esther Maria Coxe, the daughter of a prominent Philadelphia physician. Esther came to live at Woodlawn and was a devoted friend to Nelly. Lawrence Lewis bought a second plantation, Audley, in Clarke County, Virginia, which subsequently developed as the main source of income for the family. Eventually Lorenzo and Esther came to make Audley their home, but the families moved back and forth between the two plantations and spent a great deal of the time together.

In 1829, the Butlers returned to the east when Gen. Gaines resumed the eastern command. During the next two years Parke lived with her mother at Woodlawn, and her husband alternated between Woodlawn and army headquarters. The housekeeping book was probably begun at this time, and most of the entries were made. Nelly was extremely happy to have all her children with her, in addition to her first two grandsons, George Washington Lewis and Edward G. W. Butler, Jr. She was as doting as a grandmother as she was a mother.

Unfortunately for her peace of mind, Edward Butler decided that the difficulties of obtaining advancement in a peacetime army were insuperable. He determined to resign his commission and take up sugar planting in Louisiana. One of his sisters had settled there, and the opportunities for an ambitious young man to make his fortune were reputed to be excellent. Nelly was horrified, considering Louisiana a primitive frontier outpost lacking the comforts and elegancies of life in Virginia. Nevertheless, the Butlers became permanent residents of Dunboyne Plantation, Iberville Parish, Louisiana, to Nelly's constant lament. She never forgave Edward for taking her daughter so far away, and she came to think of him as a monster of selfishness. He returned her dislike and considered her meddlesome. Two imperious and jealous natures clashed and could not get along.

Nelly was also disappointed in her plans for Angela. Because of Agnes's death, she could not bring herself to send her baby daughter away to school. She suggested to her husband that she and Angela move to Philadelphia or Washington during Angela's school years so that Angela could attend school as a day student, and Nelly could enjoy the pleasures of city life. Lawrence was not only appalled at the suggestion, but the Lewises' finances could not stretch so far. Instead they took a cottage in Alexandria during the winter, and Angela took private lessons with a Quaker schoolmaster who kept a school in the city. Nelly attended the recitations and herself studied Spanish with a tutor.

In 1834, she and Angela went to visit Parke in Louisiana; there Angela met and became engaged to Charles Conrad, a New Orleans attorney who later became prominent in state politics. Despite his place of residence, Nelly was charmed with the young man and agreed to their marriage in 1835. She could not, however, bear to be separated permanently from Angela and came to spend most of her time with the Conrads. They lived in New Orleans during the winter, but during the unbearably hot summer the women, and later the children, moved to the Gulf Coast town of Pass Christian, Miss. During the next four years Nelly generally lived in Louisiana with brief returns to Woodlawn. Lawrence, in increasingly feeble health, visited Louisiana and, for a time, thought of settling there, but he came to spend most of his time with his son at Audley. The Lewises were not estranged, but their tastes were so dissimilar that they were happier apart.

These were the melancholy years of the decline of Woodlawn, as it ceased being profitable and was allowed to decay. To some extent, the story of the decline of Woodlawn is part of the story of the general decline of Virginia plantation agriculture. Land, which had been fertile and productive in the colonial period, had been depleted by poor agricultural practices. Virginia could no longer compete with the new plantation areas opening in the western states, where virgin soil produced crops abundantly and cheaply, without the need for time-consuming and expensive fertilization.

The area around Alexandria, in particular, had fallen on hard times. Alexandria was no longer the thriving port city which George Washington had known. The grandiose scheme of building a canal connecting the Potomac with the Ohio River, in which Washington had invested heavily, had failed. It would have opened up the trade of the Ohio Valley and have made Alexandria a major national port, but its failure doomed any chance for Alexandria to develop. During the Napoleonic wars the capture of many American ships in the West Indies had caused a number of disastrous failures and bankruptcies among Alexandria merchants. The city had been captured during the War of 1812 by the British and had been forced to pay high indemnities. A yellow fever epidemic in 1803 and a cholera epidemic in 1832 had caused many deaths and disrupted the foreign trade which had been the life blood of the city. Two major fires in 1810 and 1824 had done considerable damage to warehouses and wharf facilities. This litany of disasters had changed Alexandria from a bustling, growing port city into a minor backwater to the detriment of all the planters in the area.

Lawrence Lewis was unfortunately not a successful or ambitious planter; that indolence which Washington had observed and criticized in him as a young man characterized his farming endeavors. He was not interested in farming as Washington had been; he did not study and experiment with new agricultural techniques and did not try out new seeds and crops. He was a planter because he owned land, but had no real enthusiasm for the role. He also suffered a great deal of ill health. By the 1820s he suffered from chronic gout, spending weeks at a time in bed with his afflicted legs and head wrapped in silk handkerchiefs, unable to leave the room or to attend to his affairs. He also had weak eyes and sometimes found it difficult to read or to examine figures or his account books.

By 1835, Woodlawn, so far from being profitable, had begun to eat up the profits from Audley and other investments. Little by little, attempts to farm the land were abandoned; fields were given over to weeds, although the house was maintained; and the remaining slaves were divided among the three surviving children. The financial failure of Woodlawn had much to do with the bitterness of Lawrence Lewis's last days. He tended to blame Nelly's extravagance and folly for many of the family's financial problems. Certainly Nelly enjoyed travel, entertaining, and maintaining the standard of living to which she had been brought up, but she could hardly be blamed for the failure of the plantation. Nelly herself always spoke of her aging and testy husband with respect, but there was clearly a lack of sympathy in their dispositions.

Nelly returned to Woodlawn for a brief visit in 1839; while she was away, Angela became ill unexpectedly and died. The shock was compounded by the death two months later of Lawrence Lewis. Nelly was totally distraught. She made a brief attempt to live with the Butlers, but this scheme could not succeed because she and Edward Butler were so incompatible. In 1840, she took up permanent residence at Audley with Lorenzo and Esther Lewis and their six sons. Her grandchildren became the major interest of her life. Besides the Lewis boys, the two Conrad boys spent long periods of time at Audley with their grandmother. Three of the Butler children went to school in the east and also visited her frequently.

Her later years were pleasant as she enjoyed good health, although punctuated with bouts of hypochondria, and a calm existence on a beautiful plantation. Although Audley was more isolated than Woodlawn, relatives and friends visited regularly. Nelly continued to delight in travel. She often made extended visits to her sister in Georgetown and to other relatives. She sometimes spent the summer in Newport with Charles Conrad, who had remained a close friend, and her grandchildren. With the election of Zachary Taylor as President, she also found a friend in the White House who treated her with the deference that made it a pleasure for her to visit there.

Despite failing eyesight and the need for glasses, Nelly continued to do fine needlework until the end of her life. She delighted in making bookmarks, pictures, firescreens, and pillow covers as gifts for her many friends and relatives. She continued to have a lively interest in cultural and world affairs and regularly read histories, biographies, poetry, and novels.

Sad events darkened the last few years of her life. Woodlawn, by now a ghostly relic, was sold in 1846. Lorenzo died very suddenly in 1847; Nelly continued to live with her beloved daughter-in-law, Esther. In 1850, she suffered a stroke which left her partially paralyzed and dependent on a wheelchair. Nevertheless, she continued to be active and interested in her friends and hobbies. On July 15, 1852, Nelly died at Audley. She was buried at Mount Vernon with her husband and her daughter, Angela. She had finally come home.

Housekeeping Book

Manuscript housekeeping books were kept by many Virginia housewives from colonial days on. These books are the source of much of the information we have today about early food and recipes. Ladies would add interesting or unusual recipes as they came across them; often they were no more than memory aids, a listing of ingredients with no techniques or specific instructions because those would be apparent to the experienced cook. Only an unusual dish, such as a delicate pudding or elaborate cake, would be cooked by the mistress of the plantation herself; slave cooks did almost all the cooking. In using either these books or the printed cookbooks which were becoming common, the recipes would be read aloud to illiterate servants. Housekeeping books were also used in training the daughters of the family in household management, and along with published cookbooks, were passed down by mothers to their daughters as part of their family heritage.

Mrs. Lewis used a bound volume with unlined blank paper for her recipes. Its cover is old marbled boards, half bound in calf. It is octavo in twelves with wove paper, measuring 19.9 cm. × 16.9 cm. × 2.5 cm.

The book is divided into two parts—starting at opposite ends of the volume with sections back to back and upside down in relation to one another, separated in the middle of the book by blank pages. This scheme was a common practice in English housekeeping manuscripts which was carried over to the American colonies. A Custis family heirloom manuscript cookbook, published as *Martha Washington's Booke of Cookery*, was organized in this fashion; one section contained mostly cookery recipes, and the opposing section contained stillroom directions. This book was given to Nelly Lewis by her grandmother after her marriage and may have influenced her decision to organize her own housekeeping book in such a way. However, there is no clear indication of any organizational scheme dividing recipes into two different types. Cookery predominates in the first section of the book, but it also includes a number of medical remedies and household instructions. The second portion contains more medical remedies and instructions for various crafts, but also contains food recipes. Mrs. Lewis may well have written the book in such a way just for its curious appearance with no particular idea of organization in mind.

The inside front cover denoted here as the front of the book is inscribed in Mrs. Lewis's hand, E. P. Lewis 1830. This was possibly a formal commencement of the book. On the same page are pasted two newspaper clippings on preservation techniques. There is also a pencil notation in Mrs. Lewis's hand—$62 due F.P.B. (Frances Parke Butler) Jany 7th 1830—which further aids in dating the book. The facing page is filled with scribbled notations of dosages for precipitated sulphur to prevent excessive salivation and for Seidlitz powders. There is a laundry list dated 13th Augt, 1830.

The recipes begin on the next page and run consecutively for one hundred forty-seven recipes. They are written in ink, generally in Mrs. Lewis's hand. A few are in the hand of her daughter Parke, and others are in unknown hands, written on separate pieces of paper, cut out, and pasted in the book. At random points newspaper clippings, usually dealing with food preservation or laundry methods, are pasted in.

There follow thirty-four blank pages. In the middle of the book a poem was penciled in, apparently at a later period. Then there are forty-one more blank pages.

On the opposite side of the book, upside down, the second group of recipes begins, comprising twenty-five recipes. There are a number of penciled notations inside the back cover, including notes of debts, one of which has an 1828 date, the price paid for cabbages, and lists of barnyard fowls. Some of them are illegible. In this section one of the recipes is dated 1832, another can be dated by evidence in a letter as 1835. The last three recipes, written in ink by Mrs. Lewis, are on two separate sheets of paper, folded and stuck in the back of the book. Also loose are a prescription and eighteen clippings, dated 1830 through 1838. Most of them deal with disease.

The book does not appear to have been added to after the 1830s, which would accord with the breakup of permanent residence at Woodlawn. There are many indications that the book was intended for Frances Parke Butler, since the book is heavily weighted toward the concerns of a Louisiana planter's wife. Mrs. Lewis may well have given the book to her daughter on one of her trips to Louisiana in the late 1830s. In any case, whether then or later, the housekeeping book came into Mrs. Butler's hands and was passed down through the Butler family until it was inherited by Richard C. Plater, Jr., Mrs. Butler's great-grandson. Mr. Plater presented it to the Historic New Orleans Collection, along with a large collection of Butler family papers, a selection of which it is intended to publish separately.

The sources of many of the recipes can be identified through notations which Mrs. Lewis added to them. Among the sources which can be identified are relatives and friends, servants, doctors and a pharmacist, a published cookbook, and newspapers. The numbers in the margin refer to recipe numbers, which were added by the editor.

145
27, 80
43
Mrs. Lewis's grandmother, Martha Washington, provided the remedy for worms. Although only initials were noted, the Mrs. M.L.C. who gave Mrs. Lewis the recipes for rolls and oil mangoes was probably her sister-in-law, Mary Lee Custis (Mrs. G.W.P. Custis). She received a recipe for gingerbread from Betty Lewis

84, 139
Carter (Mrs. Charles Carter), Lawrence Lewis's sister. She got two recipes for preserving green peppers from her son's mother-in-law,

69
Mrs. John Redman Coxe. It is possible, although there is no evidence to support the supposition, that the Mrs. P. who donated a sponge cake recipe might be Mrs. Lewis's sister, Martha Custis Peter (Mrs. Thomas Peter).

8, 67
174, 175
Mrs. Lewis's niece, Mary Custis Lee (Mrs. Robert E. Lee), was the source of a number of recipes. She is identified in the manuscript with gingerbread and black cake. It seems almost certain that she also provided the recipes for currant and grape wines. An identical currant wine recipe appears in *Housekeeping in Old Virginia*, where it is described as having been copied by the author from a handwritten recipe belonging to Mrs. Lee. In Mrs. Lewis's book the grape wine appears on the same loose sheet of paper with the currant wine, and both clearly seem to have been taken down at the same time from the same person.

52-54
57
60-63
Although lacking any identification in the manuscript, several cake recipes are identical with those appearing in a 1931 publication, *The Old Washington Recipes*. They were taken from a manuscript cookbook which was originally kept by a member of the Washington family and had been passed down through the Washington family to a great-great-grandniece of George Washington. Unfortunately, the authors did not identify the original compiler of the recipes. It is fascinating, but fruitless, to speculate about which member of the Washington family it was. She was clearly in close communication with Mrs. Lewis since they shared so many recipes. There are a number of indications that the Washington recipes were the originals which were copied by Mrs. Lewis. The Washington recipes have much more complete directions for preparation. In two cases there are discrepancies between the two groups of recipes with reversed numbers or ingredients left out, and in both cases the Washington recipes are correct; as, for example, in the proportions of ingredients used in the pound cake.

36
138
The medical remedies and prescriptions which are identified came from three men. Dr. D. T. Jenifer was a physician in Charles County, Maryland, in the 1830s. Dr. James Henderson was a

65
founding member of the Medical Society of Virginia and a promi-

nent physician with a large practice in Manchester, Virginia. 152–4
Edward Stabler was a pharmacist who founded the Leadbetter Drug
Store in Alexandria. His store was highly thought of, and his cus-
tomers included members of the Custis, Washington, Lewis, and
Lee families.

There is no conclusive evidence as to the identities of the
many acquaintances who gave Mrs. Lewis recipes for her book.
Some of the names simply cannot be identified at all. The following
are possibilities, but should be put no higher than that. They are
suggested because they were friends or neighbors of members of the 1
family during the relevant period. The William B. Harrison who 34
contributed a method for preserving butter might be William Butler Harrison of Loudoun County. Mrs. Barry who gave the recipe
for stewed beef could be Mrs. James A. Barry of Alexandria; her 140
husband was an acquaintance of G. W. P. Custis. Mrs. Waite who 172
provided a recipe for gingerbread might be Mrs. Obed Waite; her
husband was mayor of Winchester, 1824–1831. Mrs. Talcott of the
painting directions was very likely Mrs. Andrew Talcott; she and
her husband were married in Norfolk in 1832 and were close
friends of the Robert E. Lees.

A number of recipes apparently came from servants—both
slave and free. Attempts to identify them positively from 141,143
Woodlawn records, however, were unsuccessful. Clearly Old Doll, 158
Old Letty, and Dolcey were slaves; a Dolcy, perhaps the same per- 36,85,87
son, was listed among the slaves belonging to the Butlers during the
1830s. Hanson was probably a male slave cook; it was quite common to have male cooks since it was believed that they could with-
stand the scorching heat of fireplace cooking better than women 88,132
could. The Clements would seem to have been free white em- 142
ployees. The lack of an honorific with Clement's name shows that
he was considered socially inferior, but the use of "Mrs. Clement" 79
argues that they were not slaves. Ann Bamber was a white servant
who was much esteemed by the Lewis family. Frances Butler tried
to employ her as a baby nurse in the late 1820s, but by that time she
had entered a convent in Kentucky.

A number of recipes and discussions on disease came from
newspapers, but only two papers can be positively identified. The 18,150
source of the recipes for furniture polish and protection of bee hives
was the *American Farmer*, a paper endorsed by such American
leaders as Jefferson and Madison; it was devoted to rural economy,
internal improvements, news, and valuable and eclectic information. It was founded and published by John S. Skinner, the postmas-
ter of Baltimore; he also served as editor from 1819 to 1829. The 134
discussion on consumption was taken from the *Boston Medical and*

Oil portrait of Nelly Custis Lewis, by Beale Bordley, 1832. Courtesy Kenmore Association, Inc.

Surgical Journal. Devoted to medical news, it was formed in early 1828 by joining two earlier medical journals.

91-131

Although not identified by Mrs. Lewis, the source of the largest block of recipes in the manuscript was *The French Cook* by Louis Ude, a popular cookbook of the period. Mrs. Lewis copied forty recipes for soups, sauces, and desserts. Since she copied the recipes, the book probably did not belong to her. Their being copied in sequence suggests that she probably encountered the book on a visit and copied the recipes during the limited time that the book was available to her.

Household Management and Cookery

The mistress of a large estate, such as Woodlawn, faced a formidable administrative task in feeding her family and guests every day. She had to see to the preparation and serving of an enormous dinner in addition to the other smaller meals. Dinner was expected to be both abundant and elegant in appearance. As an added complication, she was never quite sure how many would sit down to dinner, since it was quite acceptable for unexpected guests to arrive at dinnertime or for her husband to bring home ten or twelve guests without warning.

Thus the food supply was one of her major concerns. She had to be sure that the smokehouse was full of meat, that sufficient flour had been milled and stored free from bugs and mold, that butter was churned, that the chicken yard contained enough laying hens to provide the enormous number of eggs used in dessert and sauce cookery, that a supply of fresh fowls, fish, shellfish, and game was available, that the garden and orchard were sufficient for fresh produce and preservation, that the cellar was filled with preserves, jams, pickles, and preserved vegetables, and that imported luxuries such as tea, coffee, sugar, spices, salt, and wine were purchased and properly stored.

Rotten—literally rotten—food was a hazard for the hostess attempting to provide delicious, abundant, and varied meals. There was no refrigeration, and commercially canned foods were not considered acceptable for a discriminating diner. Meat, more than any other food, caused problems with its rapid spoilage. Chickens and other birds, fish, shellfish, and lamb could be consumed within twenty-four hours so that preservation was not necessary. However, cattle and hogs provided a mountain of meat which could not possibly be eaten before it spoiled. Even though people in the nineteenth century ate a great deal of meat that was very "high" and today would be considered spoiled, there was a limit to what could possibly be eaten with safety. Pork especially presented health hazards if not properly cared for.

Drying and pickling were processes for meat preservation that were sometimes used, but the most common means of preservation was salting. Dry salting, burying the meat in a bed of powdered salt, was effective but expensive, so that the most common method involved making brine, a salt and water solution, and soaking the meat in it.

Getting a supply of good salt was in itself a problem in

America. Most of the world's supply of salt at the time was made by evaporating sea water, but it varied widely in effectiveness depending on the quality of the water used and the methods used in its preparation. Low salinity made attempts to dry American bay water for salt ineffective, so most salt was imported from Europe. The preferred high quality salt for the table was imported from Lisbon, but a cheaper grade of English salt was often used for salting meat.

Most slaughtering was done in late fall when cool weather had set in to avoid the heat and to save food costs for the animal over the winter. A small amount of slaughtering was also done in the early spring. Beef and pork were the only meats salted in any quantity in Virginia. Mutton and venison tasted bad when salted and so were only eaten fresh. Salt fish, which was eaten in the north, was considered fit only for slaves.

A careful hand with salting was essential. Good quality salt was essential, as bad salt would make the meat very hard. Saltpeter, more drying and penetrating than salt, was added to give the meat its characteristic red color. Without it, salted meat would have been a washed-out unappetizing gray color. Care had to be taken not to add too much of the chemical, however, for too much saltpeter would turn the brine green and make the meat very dark and hard. Sugar or molasses was often added for flavor and to prevent the meat from becoming too tough. Spices were also added sometimes for flavor.

After steeping for some weeks in the brine, the pieces of meat would be taken out and rubbed with further drying ingredients, such as wood ash, and then hung in the smokehouse. The smokehouse at Woodlawn is a separate brick building with a stone floor. A smoky fire would be made up daily to further preserve the meat. Treated this way, meat easily lasted throughout the year and provided a constant source of meat for the table. Virginia bacon and hams were famous delicacies.

Shellfish, particularly oysters, were enjoyed fresh, but were also valued because they could easily be pickled and saved for later use without the extensive salting operations necessary for red meats. Virginia housewives were well aware of the importance of boiling food before it could be bottled. Boiling vinegar and spices, especially cayenne pepper, acted as preserving agents.

Maintaining a constant source of vegetables was an important concern for any hostess. It has sometimes been mistakenly assumed that vegetables were less commonly eaten in the nineteenth century or that they were badly cooked. Vegetable recipes were often neglected in cookbooks because it was assumed that everyone knew how to cook them properly. Indeed, even in winter, dinner

28,30

33

always included a large assortment of vegetables to complement the meat dishes. Planting successive crops and the use of garden glasses and hotbeds provided fresh vegetables for the household from spring through early fall. But preservation for the cold months to assure a continuing supply was important. Root vegetables, such as potatoes, carrots, and radishes were put down in layers of dry sand in the cellar. Cabbages and cauliflowers were buried in earth and covered with straw. Corn, peas, and beans were dried and put in containers. Onions and garlic were dried and strung in the air.

Soft and easily spoiled vegetables, however, needed further treatment if they were to be fit for human consumption throughout the winter months. Although commercial canning of food in tin containers had begun, spreading from England to the United States in 1819, canned goods were still not widely used, not being considered as good nor as safe as home-processed foods.

Containers for home canning included glass bottles, wide-mouthed glass jars, and stoneware jars. The process was the same in all cases. The vegetable was first boiled, then placed in the container and sealed airtight. Sometimes the container was sealed by pouring a layer of boiling, clarified fat over the top and then being stoppered with a waxed cork. At other times a cloth was used, over which hot melted wax was poured, or a leather or bladder which was taped closed. Sometimes bacteria did enter, so that food was always carefully examined for signs of spoilage before use, but it usually lasted quite well.

Mrs. Lewis included only one recipe for vegetable preserving of this sort. Interestingly enough, it is for tomatoes. It shows the concern felt by home canners to maintain the color and appearance of the food while rendering it safe through thorough cooking and the use of preservative spices such as ginger. 44

This collection of recipes is unusual in the large number of tomato recipes it includes. Although the tomato had originated in America, it had travelled around the world before being introduced and accepted in the United States. Brought to Europe by Spanish conquerors, the original tomato was small and golden and grew in bunched clusters. It quickly became popular in Spain and Italy where it was known as *pomodoro*, or golden apple. It was introduced into England in the 1600s, where because of a mistranslation, it was called love apple. This probably gave rise to the idea that the tomato had aphrodisiac qualities. Throughout the next two hundred years the tomato in England and the American colonies was kept largely as an ornamental garden curiosity; many people even believed that it was poisonous. The tomato began to be eaten in Virginia in the late eighteenth century, but grew slowly in popularity. By the 1830s the tomato was still somewhat out of the ordinary, although clearly relished by the Lewis family.

Vegetables were sometimes made into sauces to be used with fish or meat. One popular sauce was ketchup; it had originated as an oriental brine sauce made of pickled fish or shellfish. In English and American usage it had come to mean a condiment sauce made from any of a variety of ingredients, the most common being walnuts, anchovies, and mushrooms. Only in the nineteenth century was ketchup made of tomatoes, and it was still somewhat unusual. Mrs. Lewis's tomato ketchup would have been a highly spiced sauce, probably considerably thinner and runnier than modern ketchup.

One of the most essential products in the nineteenth-century larder was vinegar. Without it, much food preservation would have been impossible. Vinegar was an extremely ancient product; as its name indicates, it was originally made from flat or sour wine. Its preservative qualities were early recognized. Vinegar came to be made from many substances other than wine, including cider, malt or ale, brown sugar, raisins, currants, and various berries. Raspberry vinegar was a common type in Virginia.

Vegetables pickled in vinegar were an essential component of the Virginians' winter diet. They were used in winter salad, as garnishes for roast, and in stews and hashes for variety of flavor and color. Artichokes, asparagus, beans, beets, cabbage, cauliflower, walnuts, and herbs, as well as cucumbers, mushrooms and onions were commonly pickled. The pieces of vegetable were usually put in hot brine, that is, salt water, and then drained and transferred to vinegar, flavored with a variety of spices. Great care was taken to retain the texture and color of the vegetable so that it would be crisp and attractive for serving. For a yellow pickle, turmeric and sun bleaching were used. For a white pickle, white wine and white pepper were used. For a green pickle, vinegar or vine leaves were used. The two recipes for pickled green peppers show this concern to maintain a crisp texture and green color.

A popular winter preserve was India or Indian pickle, also know as pickallilli. In Mrs. Lewis's recipe the pickling liquid was very spicy with a combination of ginger, garlic, red pepper, horseradish, turmeric, and mustard seed. This, by the way, would make a yellow pickle. It called for somewhat more technique than the commoner types of pickles because of the process of adding a series of vegetables as they came into season.

Fruits, of all the varieties known in Europe as well as native American berries, were among the most popular of Virginia delicacies. However, fresh fruits have a short season and are one of the

26

most easily spoiled foods so their preservation was important to Virginia housewives. A few fruits could be stored without processing. Apples were dried or stored in barrels in the cellar, and lemons and oranges were stored in nets for some time. However, most fruits rot too quickly for such treatment to be useful. Small fruits, such as cherries, were sometimes packed tightly in glass bottles which were corked and waxed, as was done with green peas. However, for most fruits preservation with sugar was the most effective way of ensuring a continuing supply out of season.

Inferior fruits, bruised or discolored, were mashed and used to make marmalades and jams. As only currants and quince have enough natural pectin to jell by themselves, currants or isinglass would be added to make other fruits jell. Fruit juice was also used to make fruit syrup.

The preferred method was to take firm fine fruit and to preserve it whole with care to maintaining its shape and color for a handsome appearance when served. The fruit was boiled in sugar and water and drained; then the thickened syrup was poured over it, and the bottles sealed. Fruit was usually placed in glass bottles so that it could be checked for signs of fermentation or spoilage. All Mrs. Lewis's recipes follow this form. They were quite heavy-handed in the amount of sugar used because of sugar's preservative quality and because the taste of the time was for very sweet food. Ginger and citrus peels were commonly added to preserved fruits both for flavor and color. It was considered essential to preserve the color of the fruit. Green figs had their color maintained with grape and cabbage (the green outer) leaves. The recipe for crab apples calls for the use of a copper saucepan to green the fruit. The verdigris from copper would certainly green fruits and vegetables but in sufficient quantity could be extremely poisonous. Although the hazard was known, the extremely dangerous practice was quite commonplace.

2,12,15
81,89,90

A variation on the method of preserving whole fruit was the addition of brandy, most commonly with peaches. Brandy peaches were a very popular meat garnish or dessert. Sugar syrup was still an essential component of the preserving process, but with the addition of brandy for flavor. The use of lye to defuzz peaches was common and would not adversely affect the flavor of the dish.

16,74
88

Fruits were occasionally pickled with a salt solution in the same way as vegetables were done. This collection has one example, the extremely fashionable oil or melon mango. The tropical mango had been brought to England from the East in the seventeenth century; the expensive and rare jars of pickled mangoes became a faddish luxury item. Since fresh mangoes were unavailable, attempts to

80

duplicate the dish with substitutes were made, using vegetable marrows, cucumbers, onions, and peaches. However, the most common and satisfactory substitute was a small muskmelon of some sort, quite often a cantaloupe. These oil mangoes were extremely popular in eighteenth-and nineteenth-century America. They were extremely hot and spicy, similar to the India pickle, and would be used as a garnish with meat dishes, rather than as a fruit dessert.

One last method of preserving fruits was by candying them. Depending on the degree of hardness attained, candied fruits were known as confections, sweetmeats, or chips. All were similar to 144,158 modern crystallized fruit. Firm fruits such as cherries, plums, apricots, peaches, and pears were used, as well as orange and lemon peel. Fruits were first cooked in sugar syrup and then dried in the sun, being turned and having more thick syrup poured over them periodically for even crystallization. The peach chips and tomato figs in this collection would have been served, not as a part of the dessert course, but with raisins after the table had been cleared. The tomato figs demonstrate the common attempt to use one food to imitate the flavor of another.

Miscellaneous problems of preservation were presented by 1,72 butter and eggs. Cows were not always fresh and hens did not always lay, so that the provident housewife tried to keep some preserved items on hand. Butter was commonly salted to keep it from becoming rancid. The addition of saltpeter and sugar should have been effective, as both were preservative agents. Before use, the butter would have had to be carefully and thoroughly washed. Various forms of egg preservation were used, including coating their shells with paraffin and the use of lime as in this collection.

The meals served at the mansion were one of the most visible symbols of the success of a lady as a housekeeper. The Virginia planter class took its meals seriously. Dinner was the social center of the day, and people expected to sit down to an enormous meal. Every day, even during the most unbearable summer heat spell, they sat down to a dinner made up of a staggering variety of food arranged in the most original and attractive manner possible.

The dining room at Woodlawn is a lovely room with large graceful proportions. The Lewises furnished it with mahogany; the table appointments were impressive with English china and massive silver flatware. The sideboard was graced with cut glass decanters, silver candlesticks, silver coffee and tea service, and a silver wine waiter. The table was laid with linen table cloth and napkins; on it would be placed silver and crystal pickle vases, saltcellars, sugar bowls, and cruets for mustard, ketchup, and sauces.

Both sugar and salt were bought in hard form and had to be

Dining room at Woodlawn. Courtesy Woodlawn Plantation, a Property of the National Trust for Historic Preservation.

pounded in a mortar and then sifted. Salt was usually served in open bowls served with small spoons or the fingers. Sugar was placed on the table in a bottle or castor or in a small glass or silver bowl with a perforated ladle for sprinkling.

Mustard was the commonest of the spices and always appeared on the dinner table. Although prepared mustard could be purchased, it was usually made at home fresh for every meal. The very inexpensive native seeds were pounded in a mortar and moistened with vinegar. For fancier mustards, additional powdered spices, honey, or wine might be added. Mustard was used with almost any meat and incorporated into various sauces.

Dinner in Virginia was served at some time between two and four o'clock, usually at the later time at Woodlawn. It was served in two courses, following the English fashion. The first course was made up of meats and vegetables and the second of desserts and fruits. A great variety of food was served in each course, but a guest was not expected nor desired to sample every dish. Indeed quite often a dish would be rather small, capable of serving only a few people. Each guest was to choose a few favorites from among the abundance provided.

Attractive arrangement of the food on the table was just as important as cooking it well. Platters and serving bowls were to be arranged in a balanced and symmetrical manner. Top and bottom dishes were to be on matching platters, as should side dishes and diagonals. The ideal was that serving pieces should create a series of balances.

Soup was always served as part of the first course. A large tureen was placed before the hostess, who served the guests. The tureen was then removed and replaced with a main dish. A dish such as soup which was taken from the table before the end of a course was known as a "remove."

A typical first course would include a large standing cold ham wrapped in a linen napkin at the top of the table balanced by a hot saddle of mutton, leg of lamb, roast beef, turkey, or goose at the bottom of the table. The centerpiece would be, not flowers, but an elaborate main dish. It might be a mock turtle, a huge meat pie, a haunch of venison, or a "made dish," a complicated composition of meat, sauced and garnished with such ingredients as eels, chicken livers, mushrooms, oysters, and cockscombs.

Side dishes would include a number of other meats—stews, chickens, ducks, wild fowl, seafood, and fish. The meat dishes were attractively garnished with fresh parsley and other herbs, forcemeat balls, bacon curls, minced hard-boiled eggs, pickled vegetables, sliced fruit, cockscombs, and sippets, fried bread cut in fanciful shapes. Seafood and fish were plentiful and were great favorites with the Lewis family. Oysters and crabs were pickled, fried, boiled, made into soups, and combined in sauces for other meat or fish. Shad, cod, herring, and sturgeon were favorite fish. They were roasted or boiled whole with great care to maintain their shape and appearance. Many of the meats and fish had a separate sauce, gravy, or relish which would be placed in small tureens or sauce jugs next to the dish they were meant to accompany.

Salads and vegetables would be abundant among the side dishes. Both green and seafood salads were common, dressed with oil and vinegar; tomatoes, however, were seldom eaten raw in salads. Vegetables were an essential part of the meal. Colonial Virginians had imported the seeds for most European vegetables, which had become naturalized, as well as cultivating native vegetables. Most of the vegetables known to Americans today were also enjoyed in nineteenth-century Virginia. Fresh, they were usually lightly boiled and served with butter or cream sauces. Green peas in particular were considered the mark of an elegant table and were served as often as possible. Vegetables were also added to stews and made dishes and served as garnishes for many meats. In winter the mainstays of vegetable cookery were dried peas and beans, root vegetables, and various sorts of pickled vegetables. Root vegetables were often mashed with butter and spices. Potatoes and rice were commonly served among the side dishes. Italian-style pasta was a popular favorite as well; vermicelli was usually put into soup, but macaroni was often prepared as macaroni and cheese, baked and with the top browned.

The serving style was that known as French fashion. The hostess served the soup and the top dish, while the host served the bottom dish. Side dishes were served by the person seated nearest to them. The numerous maids and waiters, who at Woodlawn were considerably better trained than at many southern mansions, put the platters on the table and removed them at the end of the course and served the dessert course. They brought fresh dishes and glasses as necessary and served drinks and dishes displayed on the side board.

With the removal of the food and dishes from the first course, the table cloth was also removed, uncovering a fresh linen cloth on which the second course was to be served. In Virginia the second course was usually a true dessert course in which a stagger-ing array of sweet dishes was served. The centerpiece for this course at most elegant homes was a glass pyramid with a heavy pedestal base supporting numerous glass dishes to a height of two or three feet. On it would be arranged fruit jellies, custards, creams, and candied fruits, as well as ceramic figures and other adornments.

Top and bottom dishes would be impressive desserts such as a large iced fruit cake and a large plum pudding with sauce. Side dishes would include pies, small puddings, tarts, sweetmeats, ice creams, cold molded desserts, pancakes, doughnuts, crullers, cookies, wafers, and fresh or preserved fruit.

On a formal occasion, at the end of the second course the second cloth would also be removed, leaving the bare mahogany. Preserved fruits, raisins, and nuts would be served. Fresh glasses and tumblers were provided, and a series of toasts were drunk. On impressive occasions at Woodlawn, for the toasts Mrs. Lewis used silver tumblers which George Washington had used in military camp during the Revolutionary War.

There was no set convention about what drinks to serve with various foods. Therefore, with every course diners would be offered a wide variety of beverages to suit their tastes. Cider, rum and fruit punch, fruit cordials, coffee, tea, ale, and a variety of wines, but never water, would be offered throughout the meal. The wines would include madeira, sherry, claret, and rhenish. In accord-ance with the taste of the time for sweet wines, people added sugar lumps to wines which were not sweet enough for them.

The other meals of the day were nothing, or perhaps a relief, compared to dinner. The great amount of food served and consumed at dinner made it essential that the other meals be small. Breakfast was a light meal served between 8:00 and 9:00. Tea, chocolate, and coffee were served with some sort of hot bread—muffins, biscuits, or waffles. Leftovers from the day before often appeared as cold sliced ham, meat hashes, and fricassees.

Late afternoon tea in the English manner featured cakes, cookies, and breads. Supper was also a light meal served at 8:00 or 9:00 in the evening. Coffee, tea, and wines, including champagne, would be served, along with an assortment of cold meats, fruits, cookies, buns, small cakes, and sweets.

The amazing thing was that these elaborate and elegant meals were prepared in the most primitive of kitchen conditions. The kitchen at Woodlawn, as at most plantations, was in a separate building; this arrangement provided safety from fire and insulated the house from kitchen heat during the hot summer. The kitchen was located in one of the brick wings of the house, connected to it by a passageway. The floors would have been either brick or stone—the kitchen has not been reconstructed at Woodlawn—for safety from fire and ease in cleaning.

There were few closets or pantries. Chests and barrels were used to store bulky foods, and the cellars below the kitchen at Woodlawn served for most storage. Additional food storage was provided by the smokehouse and the ice house, both separate structures at Woodlawn. Dressers with shelves, as well as open shelves on the walls, held kitchen equipment. Tools and long-handled utensils hung from wall pegs.

The dominant feature of the kitchen was the huge brick fireplace. Although iron cookstoves were in use in Europe, they were not commonly used in this country until after 1850. Any of the recipes in this collection which mention using a cookstove were copied from the French cookbook. The utensils and cooking methods called for in the other recipes, as well as references to Woodlawn's kitchen in letters, make it plain that the Lewises did not have a cookstove but used a large open hearth.

Fireplaces were equipped with iron cranes attached to one wall of the chimney so that the cook could use different parts of the fireplace. This crane supported pothangers from which large pots and kettles were suspended over the fire. The pothangers could be raised or lowered to adjust the temperature; there were various means of doing this, most commonly with ratchets or hook-and-eye arrangements. Soups, stews, vegetables, boiled pudding, and meats were often cooked in these hanging pots. The ubiquitous

Virginia ham was commonly cooked in this way. It was first soaked in several changes of water to counteract saltiness and then simmered slowly over the fire in a pot with plenty of water and a variety of flavoring agents.

Leftover meat was commonly chopped up to be hashed or stewed in a footed pan over coals. Meat was seldom fried or grilled because these operations called for the constant attention of the cook, who was overseeing so many dishes simultaneously; they also called for leaning over the fire which was very hot and uncomfortable.

Boiling and roasting were the most common means of cooking meat. Roasting was usually done on a spit, a long wrought iron bar with prongs to hold the meat. Smaller, thinner spits were used for fowls; there were also spits with splints or baskets for fish and soft meat. In the early days a cook boy had turned the spit by a handle, but this was hot and tedious work. Carelessness and inattention by the boy would result in a large roast being scorched and spoiled. Therefore, every well-equipped kitchen had some sort of mechanical jack to turn the many spits. No doubt Woodlawn had one but there is no evidence to show which of the popular type of jack they used. Jacks were driven by clockwork weights, smoke, and winding and unwinding cords.

A long metal dripping pan was placed below the roasting meat to catch the juices for gravy. Pieces of cut-up meat and potatoes were sometimes placed in this pan to cook.

Besides being roasted on a spit, fowls were often roasted in a tin oven, a metal contraption shaped like half a cylinder with a spit set in the axis. The open side faced the fire so that the bird quickly cooked through a combination of direct heat and radiation from the rounded side of the oven.

Mrs. Lewis's recipe book is noticeably lacking in recipes for the two most important components of dinner, meats and vegetables. Salting and pickling are given some attention, but there are hardly any recipes for cooking meats and vegetables. Presumably it was felt that the cook would thoroughly understand this sort of commonplace cookery so that recipes for roasting beef or boiling peas would be completely unnecessary. *34, 98 99, 100–103*

Besides the recipe for stewed beef the only recipes for meat are those for aspic and meat jelly to garnish elegant cold meat dishes. Most meats were accompanied by sauces or gravies. Thus, it was important to collect recipes for a variety of smooth and tasty gravies.

There is only one true vegetable recipe in the whole collection, cabbage pudding. The other vegetable recipes are for pre-

14 serves, sauces and soups. Since most vegetables were boiled, recipes were not needed. The cabbage was probably included because it was unusual in its preparation.

13,35
36,41
91-97
104-107 This collection is, however, particularly rich in soups and desserts. Soup was an important element of the first course even in summer. A hostess was expected to have variety in her repertoire and not to serve the same few soups day after day. Soup was to be an elegant introduction to dinner, setting the stage for the other dishes. The visual presentation of the soup, as with all aspects of the meal, was very important. Vegetables were to be attractively cut, for example, fluted or cut into diamonds or other fancy shapes as were the sops or sippets of bread which often garnished soups.

Baked goods are the real heart of this manuscript. These were considered essentials of good eating, and there were endless variations in flavor and appearance for the many meals of the day.

Baking was even more difficult than regular meal cookery. The oven was a beehive-shaped structure of brick built alongside the fireplace. It was unflued and low-roofed with a small wrought iron door. Often there would be a small ledge in front of the oven with a hole for wood ash to drop through to be swept out at floor level.

The oven involved a great deal of labor to use and generated terrific heat in the kitchen, even beyond that of the usual roaring fire in the hearth. Therefore the oven was heated only once a week, and all major baking was done at that time. A strong fire was built on the floor of the oven very early in the morning and stoked so that it burned fiercely; the oven door was left ajar to provide oxygen for the fire. With a long stick the fire was distributed evenly over the floor of the oven; then over the next one to two hours it was allowed to burn down to a bed of coals. The coals were raked out of the oven and disposed of. The oven by this time was very, very hot because the bricks had absorbed so much heat. The oven was swept and then mopped with a wet mop; it was then ready for baking.

In the meantime all the goods to be baked that day had been prepared. Yeast breads had been allowed to rise, and all batters were in their proper pans. Baking was a highly organized, efficient operation in which none of the precious heat of the oven was allowed to go to waste.

Pies, pastries, and large loaf cakes were baked first as they needed a hot oven and short cooking time. A peel, a long-handled wooden shovel, was used to slip all the baked goods in and out of the oven without the danger of the cook's being burned.

The week's supply of bread was next placed in the oven. All the bread was packed in as tightly as necessary; it was not combined with any other baked goods. During its baking the oven was not to be opened before two hours had passed because admitting cold air to the oven would harm the bread. After the bread was removed, small cakes and tarts, biscuits, puddings, custards, and cookies would be put in batch by batch. The last bits of warmth would often be used to dry feathers, herbs, and grain, to make charcoal, and to dry kindling for the next week's baking.

A good supply of yeast was essential to successful bread making. Housewives who lived in town could purchase brewers' yeast, but on a plantation homemade yeast was a necessity. Yeast could be made from a variety of ingredients, including potatoes, peas, and malt. Hops were most commonly used in Virginia, however, as in Mrs. Lewis's recipe. Maintaining a supply of live yeast was sometimes achieved by the sourdough method, but Mrs. Lewis obviously used the method of drying the yeast with corn meal to make yeast cakes in order to preserve it.

40

Two types of bread were made—a course and substantial bread of corn meal and a more genteel bread of white flour, often with the addition of boiled rice or potatoes for moistness. Both meal and flour were stored in barrels and had to be carefully examined before use to be sure that they were free of weevils and impurities. The Lewises raised wheat and owned a grist mill so that they could be sure of a supply of fresh, unadulterated flour. Before baking, both flour and meal to be used would be sifted in trays and dried near the fire. Bread dough was often mixed in a huge wooden bread trough; in making yeast breads it was essential that the dough be kneaded at least half an hour without intermission. Both types of bread were baked in tin loaf pans, or formed into individual rolls in a skillet.

6,82
86

Many other rolls, breads, biscuits, and cookies were also baked in the oven on the weekly baking day. Philadelphia buns, bun cakes, lapland cakes, and various rolls and biscuits were made on baking day for use throughout the week, either cold or rewarmed. Some were baked in a large pan and broken; others were baked in small individual pans or dropped on a large baking sheet.

5,39,71
87,108,
132,142

Gingerbread was also baked on baking day; it was a very popular dessert and treat, which was a traditional English favorite. The most common form of gingerbread was as thin, crisp cookies. Sometimes they were rolled, cut and baked on a baking sheet. Another version was to press the dough into a fancy gingerbread mold which produced gingerbread men, or other fanciful shapes. They were baked very slowly in the cooling oven and were expected to be very crisp and thin. Baked in this way they had excellent keeping qualities and maintained their freshness for weeks. Gingerbread of

8,43

this type was excellent alone or as an accompaniment for ice creams and custards. Another form of gingerbread was more like cake; it was called soft gingerbread. It was made of leavened dough which produced a firm, dense, moist cake like modern gingerbread.

29,140

Cookies were baked in the last batch to go in the oven. They were beaten to a stiff dough, rolled thin, and cut with a cup or fancy cookie cutter. They were often pricked with a fork and dusted with sugar; they were baked on a tin sheet until very crisp, but not too brown. In the early nineteenth century cookies were known inter-changeably by the American word "cookie" and by the English word "biscuit." Biscuits in the American sense of a risen dough commonly eaten for breakfast were also eaten. A distinction was sometimes made by calling cookies "thin biscuits."

59,85

Jumbles were an adaptation of a very popular medieval English banquet cake which continued to appear in most early American cookery books. A stiff dough was shaped and baked in buttered tin plates. The original jumbles had been very elaborate interlaced knots, similar in appearance, though not in taste, to pretzels. They were pricked all over with a fork. By the nineteenth century the shape had become less elaborate; jumbles were usually formed in simple single or double ring designs. Like cookies, they were baked slowly in a cool oven. They would rise somewhat more than cookies, but would remain thin and flattish in appearance.

55

Cakes, of course, were one of the staples of the well-fed household. Baked in vast quantities, they were heavy, dense cakes which were expected to last throughout the week without becoming noticeably stale. Cakes were often used as the base for a more complex dessert; they would be topped with fruits, preserves, sauce, ice cream, or soaked in rum or brandy.

Making delicious cakes which were not heavy enough to sink a brigantine was a long and tedious process. All ingredients for cakes were to be at room temperature. It was essential to have a good grade of flour, free of bugs, dirt, and other impurities; it was always sifted and dried before baking. Leavening agents were pot-ash, pearl ash, and saleratus, as well as eggs; yeast was seldom used in dessert cakes because of its strong, sour taste. The eggs, which were an important part of cake making, had to be carefully checked for freshness. They were to be beaten thoroughly with a wooden beater; yolks and whites were usually beaten separately so that the whites could lighten the batter.

Butter, which was preserved with salt, had to be washed carefully to remove the characteristic salty taste. It was allowed to become soft and warm, but not melted, before being creamed with sugar and eggs and then added to the batter. Milk was placed in

Typical plantation kitchen. Magnolia Mound; Baton Rouge, La. Photo by Robert S. Brantley.

shallow pans, and cream was allowed to rise to the surface and skimmed off for use in cakes. The almonds so frequently called for in dessert cookery were laboriously pounded in a mortar, often with the addition of wine or rose water to keep them from oiling.

Honey had been the major sweetening agent for Europeans, but by the nineteenth century sugar had become the much overused sweetener in both Europe and the United States. Originally, sugar manufactured from sugar cane had been an expensive luxury imported from the East which only the rich could afford. However, during the centuries following the Reformation, changes in production patterns caused sugar to replace honey in European and American cooking. The monasteries had been the major producers of quantities of cheap honey from the hives they kept for the manufacture of beeswax candles. As English and continental monasteries were dissolved, the ready supply of honey fell. Coincidentally a vast expansion of sugar production occurred with the development of large sugar plantations in the Caribbean. By the nineteenth century cane sugar was widely available on the world market, although it was still rather expensive. By the 1830s, Louisiana had also opened up as a sugar planting area so that sugar was available to most

Americans; but only the well-to-do could afford the lavish use of sugar seen in these recipes.

Sugar could be purchased in a number of forms, varying in cost in proportion to the degree of refinement. Cane sugar was processed by pressing the juice from cane, treating it with lime to remove impurities, and evaporated. Molasses, the mother liquor, was removed and sold separately; it was considerably cheaper than more refined grades of sugar. It was commonly used by the poor as their major sweetener.

The next step in the sugar process was crystallizing which resulted in a crude brown sugar which was also comparatively cheap. The preferred form of sugar, however, for wealthy Europeans and Americans was the highly refined loaf sugar. Coarse brown sugar was boiled with lye or lime, skimmed of impurities, clarified with egg white and then placed in large cone-shaped molds to recrystallize and dry. Once dry, these loaves of sugar were wrapped in deep blue-purple paper and sold. As an expensive imported luxury, loaf sugar was overused by those who could afford it. A large number of very sweet dishes was the mark of an elegant dinner.

Loaf sugar was rather difficult to handle because it was very hard. Sugar for coffee, tea, or wine was cut by the mistress of the house and her daughters into nicely and regularly-shaped lumps with various sorts of sugar shears, cutters, and nippers. For cooking, great hunks of loaf sugar were cut off and pounded in a mortar, a very time-consuming task. The sugar was still full of lumps and had to be sifted before it could be used.

Spices were another commonplace product in the wealthy household. Unlike common herbs which were domesticated in the United States, spices were tropical products which always had to be imported. Although they were no longer worth the king's ransom of medieval times, they were still expensive luxuries in the early nineteenth century. Thus, as with sugar, their use signified affluence and elegance. Spices were bought whole and stored in wooden canisters. When needed, they were ground in mortars or spice mills. Nutmeg, cinnamon, ginger, and mace were the most common spices.

Spices were used much more heavily than they are today. Not only was their rich taste appreciated, but they served practical functions as well. Spices reduced the saltiness of salted meats and added zest to flavorless dried foods. Perhaps more important, they disguised the off taste of spoiled or rancid food. People in the pre-refrigeration era often ate food that today would be considered unfit for human consumption; spicy sauces and gravies masked the high taste and odor. In baking, this function was probably considerably less important.

Rose water and orange flower water were very important ingredients in baking; rose water in particular was essential, taking the place that vanilla holds today as a nearly universal baking flavor. Not only did these waters impart a delicate flavor, but they gave baked goods a very pleasant fragrance as well.

Dried fruits, such as raisins, currants, prunes, and dates, as well as citron, lemon, and orange peel were often used in baking. Raisins and prunes were stoned, and currants were washed and dried. All were dusted with flour before baking to keep them from clumping or sinking. These fruits were particularly important in holiday cooking for the great, heavy Christmas puddings and cakes that England had bequeathed to America. Even the typical wedding cake of those days was not the anemic white sugar creation of today but was much more likely to have been a sort of fruitcake.

The most common cake of the era was a large heavy cake similar in texture to a modern pound cake, often enlivened with spices and chopped fruits. Eggs were usually the major leavening agent. Once the batter was mixed, it was beaten for at least an hour without interruption. The dough was then placed in well-buttered tin pans—either a large loaf pan, a number of small pans or various fancifully-designed molds, such as the turk's head. The great cakes for festive occasions were usually iced, typically with a mixture of egg whites, sugar, and almond paste. Although cakes were usually baked in a hot oven fairly quickly, the sheer bulk of a great cake would necessitate a longer baking period of four to six hours. Typical of this sturdy cake would be the wonder, pound, composition, clove, and black cakes of this collection. In addition to these very heavy cakes leavened only with eggs were similar cakes which were somewhat lighter because of additional leavening, such as potash, pearl ash, and saleratus. These cakes were often baked in small individual pattypans, either plain or in fancy shapes, making pretty cakes for supper.

51,52
54,62
67

53,56
57,60
63,135

Sponge cake was the other major cake category; it was a much lighter, airier cake with a delicate flavor and texture. It was leavened with air incorporated into very stiffly beaten egg whites. The trick was to get as much air as possible into the whites and then carefully to fold in the other ingredients to maintain their lightness. They were baked quickly in ungreased pans in a hot oven. Coating the cake with sugar gave it a nice crust. The batter was sometimes baked in finger molds and used to surround standing creams and jellies.

7,58
68,69

In addition to oven baking, there were various sorts of fireplace baking which were done during the week. An iron Dutch oven, footed so that it could stand over coals and fitted with a flat top on which more coals were piled, was used to bake a variety of breads, cakes, pastries, and custards. For daily baking of hot breads for breakfast or supper, the griddle was most frequently used. It was a flat iron circle with a long handle by which it was suspended from a pothook in the fireplace. It was used to bake small cakes, biscuits, muffins, and crumpets. When they were left over, they would often be toasted on long forks before the fire.

3, 19
168, 169

Waffles and wafers were cooked in the fireplace. The waffle iron had a grid shape like modern waffle irons, but was mounted on a long handle; it was held over the fire and turned to bake. The wafer iron was similar to the waffle iron, but much smaller, with various ornamental designs. It had originally been used to make sacramental wafers for communion, but had passed into general usage. The wafer was a thin, crisp dessert cake like the modern vanilla wafer.

4, 61

There were also various sorts of fried cakes—doughnuts, pancakes, fritters, and crullers—which were served either at breakfast or as side dishes for dinner. Pancakes were fried either on a griddle or in a long-handled skillet. The other cakes were usually fried in deep lard in a pot hanging in the fireplace.

9, 10
31, 32
110, 111

Puddings were often served at dinner; they could be either baked or boiled although baked puddings had become by far the more common. The old English boiled or bag pudding was largely confined to the Christmas plum pudding. The baked puddings represented in this collection could have been baked in the large oven or in portable furnaces. Mrs. Lewis had two portable cast iron stoves or furnaces, similar to Dutch ovens, which were used in making confections, custards, and puddings.

38

For guests it was considered much more attractive to serve a pudding baked in a crust of puff paste. It was to be baked slowly so that the crust did not brown. For a regular family dinner, no crust was necessary and the pudding was usually baked in an earthenware container.

The method of making all the baked puddings was the same. Eggs were separated, and yolks and whites were beaten separately; the whites were added last to lighten the pudding somewhat. Puddings were made of many bases; the coconut, lemon, pumpkin, potato, orange, almond, and Indian puddings gathered in this collection were quite typical. The potatoes were probably, although not certainly, sweet potatoes; recipes of the period often failed to specify which type of potato was called for. Indian pudding made of corn meal was much more popular in New England than the south, but was eaten in Virginia.

20-25
64

Boiled puddings, except for plum pudding, were largely out of style by this time. Technique in making plum pudding was very important. Once the ingredients were mixed, the proper preparation of the bag was necessary for the success of the pudding. A very heavy linen with a close weave, called German or Russian sheeting, was used. Pudding bags were kept very clean and dry since any mustiness in the cloth would spoil the taste of the pudding. A cauldron was filled with water which was brought to a boil as the pudding was being prepared. The pudding cloth was dipped into the boiling water and then laid over a large colander or sieve which would support its heavy weight adequately. The cloth was well floured and the pudding mixture placed in the center. The opposite sides of the cloth were then knotted tightly, and the bag was suspended in the cauldron of boiling water. The bag had to remain covered at all times with constantly boiling water. Boiling water was added to the pot occasionally; the addition of cold water would make the pudding heavy and nasty tasting. After several hours of boiling, the bag was removed and opened. The hot pudding was usually served immediately.

Custards and creams were much more delicate than the heavy puddings. They were also baked in an oven slowly. Sometimes they were baked in a crust for special occasions, but usually they were baked in cups or molds. The omelette soufflé is a related dish, but it was served hot while custards were chilled before being served.

Creams were of two types. Baked creams were similar to custards with the same sort of preparation, but some variation in ingredients. Ice creams were composed of similar ingredients to baked creams, but they had a little gelatin added and were frozen over ice, rather than being baked. They were a delicacy that could be enjoyed only by those wealthy and fortunate enough to have an ice house, an agreeable luxury which many planters invested in. A circular excavation, as large as fifteen feet in diameter and fifteen feet deep was made in the ground and lined with brick. During the winter ice was cut and packed in the pit where it would last throughout the summer. A bladed ice chopper was used to cut ice as needed by the household. The Lewises had an ice house at Woodlawn, but its exact shape and size is not known because it is in ruins.

The earliest ice creams were made by placing the cream mixture in a tin pot which was buried in a pail of ice, but large ice crystals formed in the mixture. The improved ice cream freezers consisted of two pewter basins; the inside one with a top held the cream, and the outer one was packed with ice and a little salt. The ice cream was stirred at intervals with a long-handled spoon.

George Washington had bought one of the improved freezers in 1784 so Mrs. Lewis naturally was accustomed to ice cream making.

113,114
129

The commonest cream used was a custard, like the baked creams, but with the addition of isinglass to help set the mixture. Isinglass, the purest form of gelatin then available, was widely used in dessert cookery because of the fashion for molded shapes. Shaped in fancy molds, the ice creams were turned out onto plates. They were also served in glasses with handles.

121-126
130

Fromage was a similar frozen dessert. Instead of cooking milk and eggs to form an initial custard, the mixture was usually uncooked and incorporated whipped cream. Like other ice creams, it included isinglass as a stiffening agent.

147

Blancmange was another similar cold molded dessert, but it lacked the eggs of creams. Unlike a fromage, it was composed of boiled milk or cream. Its elegant white appearance and delicate flavor made it a great favorite, especially as it was usually attractively decorated with flowers, ferns, or candied violets.

Among the most popular desserts were the fruit jellies which today would be known as gelatin. They were served in little cups or shaped in molds. Tin jelly molds were sold in Virginia in a variety of shapes. They included melons, hedgehogs, stars, half-moons, sunflowers, obelisks, steeples, fish, eggs, hens, chicks, and packs of cards. A number of jellies of different colors and shapes were frequently combined to form a scene, such as a hen with chicks and eggs in a nest, or fish swimming in a pond.

112
115-120
131,146

Fruit for jelly was sweetened and usually cooked for a short while. It was considered essential to retain the bright fruit color. Clarified sugar was often used in making jelly; in clarification sugar was boiled with water and beaten egg whites, then skimmed and strained. The fruit and syrup were combined with isinglass and poured through a jelly bag, a heavy white flannel bag, into molds or cups and put on ice to become firm. Any fruit might be used to make a jelly. Most jellies were served in the dessert course, but isinglass and calves foot jellies would have been garnishes for meat in the first course. They were also considered highly desirable for invalids. They were delicate and tasty enough to tempt a wayward appetite and provided sustenance without being heavy or indigestible.

Although most of the wines consumed by the family were imported, a variety of homemade fruit wines and cordials were also served. Their extreme sweetness was thought to be especially complementary to desserts. They were also believed to have therapeutic value, serving as a tonic and appetite stimulant for people who were ailing or depressed.

All the cordials had a base of fresh fruits; almost any fruit could be used. The fruit was heavily sweetened and combined with alcohol, usually brandy or whiskey. The mixture was stored in wooden casks in the cellar during the fermentation process; when the liquid was drawn off, it was often reprocessed and then stored in large bottles or jars.

50,73
148,174
175

Medical Practices

Because the causes of most diseases were still unknown in the nineteenth century, so were their cures. Misinformation and mistaken theories led to rigorous, painful, and sometimes fatal treatments. Essentially, most patients recovered from illness because of the natural recuperative power of the human body, not because of the medical assistance they received. Nevertheless, in a period when epidemic disease was rampant, patients turned to doctors and home remedies with pathetic hope.

Doctors were most effective in dealing with wounds and other external injuries. A simple fracture could usually be set successfully. Compound fractures, however, were treated by amputation, a traumatic but life-saving process in the days before anesthesia. Skin cancers and tumors could be removed effectively although the operations caused some scarring.

Any sort of surgery resulted in infection since the importance of sterile treatment of wounds and incisions was not understood. Surgeons with dirty hands and improperly cleaned instruments moved from case to case, trailing infection in their wake. Thus all surgical incisions were expected to become infected in the normal course of healing; alarm was felt only if they became truly septic. Relatively straightforward modern surgical procedures, such as those for appendicitis, gallstones, and childbirth complications, were impossible at that time. The inevitable introduction of infection into the abdominal cavity was always fatal.

Small wounds were usually treated at home with poultices, such as tobacco or spiderweb, or bathed by a doctor with caustic substances which caused them to scar over. Very large or deep wounds were much more dangerous and difficult because so long as they remained open severe infection and gangrene might set in. The effective, if painful, treatment was to cleanse the wound and then to cauterize it with a hot iron or poker. The resulting scar was usually quite ugly.

Internal medicine was based on Galen's theory that the body was composed of four principal humors, that is, fluids: blood, phlegm, yellow bile, and black bile. The basic cause of disease was believed to be an imbalance of humors; therefore the goal of medical treatment was to restore the proper and healthful balance of these internal fluids. All internal treatment then was an attempt to build up a deficient fluid or to extract an excessive one, or perhaps both, depending on the diagnosis.

The building up process was less obnoxious than extraction since it was accomplished through the administration of drugs or an alteration in diet. It was based to a large extent on the doctrine of signatures or similars; healing herbs and foods were believed to have been marked by God for man's guidance. Therefore plants with liver-shaped leaves were useful for bilious diseases. Plants with milky juices, such as lettuce, almonds, or figs, were considered valuable in producing milk in nursing mothers. Red wines were prescribed for pallor or listlessness. Cordials bolstered a faint heart. The task of the healer was to discover what fluid was out of balance and to supply the appropriate drugs and foods. Although these treatments were not always helpful, at least they were not harmful. A number of very effective natural drugs had been discovered and were commonly used—laxatives, wormkillers, astringents, painkillers, and emollients. Fortunately for the patient, by the nineteenth century the vilest components of the pharmacopeia had fallen into disuse so that the hapless patient was no longer forced to imbibe animal blood, powdered bats' wings, urine, or toad's tongue. Although much of the medicine was no more effective, it was no longer disgusting.

The processes of extracting bodily fluids which were considered to be in excess earned for nineteenth-century medicine the sobriquet of heroic medicine. The common methods were bloodletting, purging, blistering, and inducing vomiting; in all treatments, fluids were caused to leave the body. Bloodletting (phlebotomy) was one of the favored treatments in almost any illness; it was considered particularly effective with fever, which was believed to be caused by an excess of blood. In minor cases leeches were applied, but when it was judged expedient to extract greater quantities of blood the doctor cut a vein, usually in the patient's arm and allowed him to bleed into a basin; in cases of intractable fever the patient would be bled repeatedly.

44

Blistering was particularly unpleasant. The skin was burned with a corrosive substance, such as a mustard plaster, or a hot iron so that large blisters were raised. Repeated applications were sometimes made until the patient's arms were covered with blisters.

In especially puzzling cases a combination of all four methods might be used to the extreme discomfort of the patient. George Washington's fatal illness was a good example of this sort of treatment. The sudden and severe throat and chest congestion he contracted might well have proved fatal in any case, but the continuous bleeding, purging, vomiting, and blistering he endured at the hands of his devoted physicians undoubtedly rendered his last hours hideous.

Many epidemic diseases swept the country during the nineteenth century and were particularly frightening because of their high death rates and impossibility of cure. Because causes were unknown, treatments could only be ameliorative, not curative. In fact, the very names of diseases were confused. A number of recurring fevers, including typhus and typhoid, were lumped together and known as intermittent fevers. Many forms of tooth and gum disease were known as scurvy. Diphtheria was often referred to as croup or putrid sore throat.

The common diseases of the Virginia tidewater were typhoid, typhus, yellow fever, malaria, smallpox, diphtheria, and pneumonia. Because disease was so prevalent, it was a matter of overwhelming concern. Letters and diaries were filled with notes on the prevailing symptoms and illnesses of family members, neighbors, and slaves. Table conversation among the most elegant people often turned on the current fevers, chills, and fluxes being suffered by the guests.

The specific diseases mentioned in the housekeeping book were consumption, croup, scurvy, and cholera. Consumption, as tuberculosis was generally known in the nineteenth century, was an especially dreaded disease because of its fatality. The frequent remissions which occurred in the disease, however, sometimes gave hope that specific treatments were leading to a cure. In its most common form a disease of the lungs, tuberculosis was thought of as a cold, wet disease which could be cured by applying warm, dry remedies which would dry up the hemorrhages and coughs associated with the disease. Mrs. Lewis clearly copied her description of the inhalation of nitric acid from a newspaper. It is very doubtful that she ever put such a painful treatment into effect.   134

Croup or putrid sore throat was an endemic illness, striking particularly hard at children, to whom it often proved fatal. In fact, most of these cases were probably diphtheria. Mrs. Lewis's remedy   137 involved a combination of astringent ingredients with harsh, pungent odors; it was probably intended to serve as an expectorant and to help clear the breathing passages.

Scurvy is a disease caused by a deficiency of vitamin C; among its unpleasant symptoms are sore and swollen gums, loose teeth, and foul breath. Scurvy was a common disease of the nineteenth century caused by improper diet, lacking in fresh fruits and vegetables; it is extremely unlikely that the Lewises with their varied and abundant diet would have had scurvy. However, a variety of gum and tooth diseases were known as scurvy because of the similarities of their symptoms. Mrs. Lewis's remedy included astringents to close lesions and emollients to soothe painful areas.

A nonfatal form of cholera had long been common in the United States and was treated much like the modern cold with bed rest and chicken soup. Asiatic cholera, however, was a very different disease. Native to India, cholera was a highly contagious, often fatal, disease which in the 1820s became epidemic, spreading throughout the Asian continent. As the disease moved relentlessly through Europe, reaching England in the fall of 1831, Americans braced themselves for its inevitable appearance on this continent. In June 1832, the first cases of cholera in America appeared in the port of New York; the disease quickly reached epidemic proportions in the eastern United States. In Virginia doctors and nurses were alerted; cholera hospitals were set up; and major city cleaning operations were carried out. By the end of July 1832, cholera had reached tidewater Virginia and in August broke out in Alexandria. It continued across the country during the course of the following year. In Virginia thousands of people contracted the disease, with slaves being particularly vulnerable. Although the actual death rate was only about one in three, the psychological effect was devastating. The horror and dread caused by this epidemic created a pathetic desire to believe in any reported cure. Mrs. Lewis collected her reported cures from accounts of European methods, but naturally they would have been completely useless.

Besides the terrifying epidemic diseases, the regular diseases of human life—childhood illnesses, colds, flu, stomach aches, and various fevers—plagued the Lewises. The Lewises' doctors were personal friends and regular guests at Woodlawn. In any serious illness the doctor would be called from Alexandria; because of the distance involved, he would often remain a few days, examining anyone who was ill. Ordinarily, however, because of the relative isolation and self-sufficiency of the plantation, the lady of the house was expected to dispense medicine and to deal with minor illness or with emergencies.

154

36

164, 165

Mrs. Lewis included two remedies for snakebite among her 133,136
recipes; the Butler family's removal to Louisiana caused her to feel a
great deal of anxiety about the safety of the children because of the
prevalence of poisonous snakes there. The theory behind the two
remedies was the same: to disinfect the wound with such common
cleansers as lime, chlorine, or ammonia, and then to neutralize the
poison. Although totally useless, neither remedy would have been
harmful. No remedy for snakebite could have been effective, other
than to make unbitten relatives feel useful, until the development of
modern antitoxins. The survival of the victim depended on the species of snake, the amount of poison injected in proportion to body
weight, and the position of the bite. Since snake bites are not neces-
sarily fatal, the survival of some patients probably encouraged the
belief in the efficacy of the remedies employed.

She also included two remedies for mad dog bite; perhaps 153,155
some incident in the neighborhood triggered this particular anxiety.
As in snakebite, the procedure was to disinfect the wound and then
attempt to neutralize the poison. Disinfecting a dog bite would, of
course, have been a good policy although using a corrosive substance
to dislodge a scab would have been painful. The survival of the patient would have been entirely dependent on whether the dog was
actually rabid; if infected with hydrophobia, the victim would have
been doomed since no remedy of the day could possibly have had
any effect.

The mistress of the household was expected to have a wide
knowledge of common herbal and mineral remedies and to admin-
ister them to the family and slaves. Most European medicinal plants
had been imported by the earliest settlers, had run wild and become
naturalized by this time. Early settlers had also adapted many of the
native plants known to be used by Indians for healing purposes, and
these had also by the nineteenth century become part of the home
medicine stock. Mrs. Lewis probably also owned, as Martha Washington and other family members were known to have possessed, a
medicine chest, complete with weights, scales, and knives for preparing pills. She was a frequent customer of Edward Stabler, the
Alexandria pharmacist, buying such drug staples as castor oil and
ipecac.

In the housekeeping book Mrs. Lewis collected remedies for 37,66
sore throat, ring worm, lumps in the breast, nose bleed, coughs and 138,145
colds, worms, and prescriptions for faintness and to cause vomiting. 152,157
This by no means represents a full array of the illnesses, nor of the 159,163
drugs and remedies, which she would have encountered in her daily 173
round. The remedies seem to have been randomly jotted down.
There is a wide range of usefulness among them, as might be imag-

ined. The worm remedy, for example, employed an effective wormkiller along with a natural laxative. The sore throat remedies were largely astringent, probably intended to heal inflamed tissues. A number of the remedies seem harsh, such as pepper gargle or putting vitriol in the nose.

Dentistry was, if anything, a more backward profession than medicine. The dentist was also known as a toothdrawer, which indicated his major activity. Strong wrists were essential for a dentist pulling the teeth that were so rotten and tormenting that patients could no longer bear the misery. Extraction was very painful without any anesthesia other than alcohol, but was often the only option. The dentist also sold dental paste, filled hollow teeth with gold or lead, and treated diseased gums, often by cauterizing them.

Tooth problems were endemic among Americans, who often were partially or wholly toothless by their forties; European observers commented with amazement on the phenomenon, often attributing it to the Americans' strange habit of eating hot breads. More likely, however, it could be attributed to Americans' habit of eating huge amounts of sugar, molasses, and honey in or on all their food. In addition, their general tooth care habits were deplorable.

166   Wealthy people like the Lewises were concerned with personal hygiene, cleaning their teeth and gums with such products as chlorine tooth wash. Poorer people took no care of their teeth at all, beyond an occasional gargle with rum or cider.

Extraction was not only horribly painful in itself, but the false teeth available were uncomfortable and unattractive. They were made of animal teeth, particularly those of the hippo; wood; or the teeth of other people. They were held in the mouth with springs and wires which resulted in the dour expression so typical of George Washington and others who wore false teeth.

There was naturally a great desire under the circumstances 161,162   to retain teeth as long as possible. Both Mrs. Lewis's toothache remedies had the intent of saving at least part of the tooth. Stuffing the tooth cavity with caustic substances might retard further decay and allow the dead tooth to remain in the mouth. In the more extreme case, the tooth was to be sacrificed by being cut off, but the root was to be retained to act as a base for a screwed-in substitute. Both would have hurt, but no more so than any other dental procedure.

Cosmetics and beauty products were an adjunct of the pharmacy in the nineteenth century. The pharmacist made up some of the preparations himself; more exotic and expensive products were imported from Europe. He sold a variety of soaps, shampoos, lotions, and creams. Some cosmetics were still made at home. One
70

example is the hand cream made with lard and sassafras. The lard would have been soothing and emollient; sassafras would have imparted a pleasant odor and was also believed to have medicinal qualities.

American women had never worn make up to the extent that Europeans did; the United States from its inception had been considerably more puritanical than Europe in this respect. The heavily painted and lacquered faces of the eighteenth century had given way to only the most subtle of complexion aids. A little rice powder for a shiny face and very discreet touches of rouge for cheeks and lips were used. Mrs. Lewis's lip salve was soothing and softening, and also provided a little color; the alkanet in the recipe would give it a pleasing pink shade. The effect would be much like modern lip gloss, shiny and lightly colored.

Clothing and Clothes Care

As in feeding all the plantation residents, providing clothing for them presented certain logistical problems. The Lewis family dressed well, but the styles of the 1830s did not have the richness of those worn by the Washington family. Hoop skirts were no longer fashionable, but stays, after a brief disappearance, were again required for a lady, along with wide skirts, numerous petticoats, and extremely full sleeves. Wide lace collars, called berthas, were worn as well as many shawls. Men wore frock coats, tight-fitting breeches, waistcoats, and high-standing cravats. Children wore smaller versions of adult garb.

The many slaves also had to be clothed, albeit roughly, and material provided for household needs—cooking, scrubbing, towels, sheets, draperies, bedspreads, and furniture covering.

The finest clothing was imported from Europe or from the north, as well as better grades of fabric. However, as the Lewises became comparatively poorer, they tended to rely more on local seamstresses. A considerable amount of sewing was done on the plantation itself. Although Mount Vernon's large-scale production of homespun for slave garments was not continued, large amounts of coarse cotton and linen cloth were purchased and made by slave seamstresses into the smocks or shifts worn by women and the pants and shirts worn by men. Slave seamstresses also made simple dresses for the ladies of the household. The wife of the overseer usually supervised these tasks, but the mistress of the household also had to know how things were properly done.

Girls were trained in needlework from earliest childhood. Ladies were expected to excel in ornamental needlework of various sorts, such as crewelwork, embroidery, and needlepoint. Their creations decorated the household as bell pulls, chair covers, and fireplace shields. In addition, they were expected to master plain sewing, to hem napkins and sheets, to mend, to cut a pattern, and to make simple clothes. They actually did a good deal of the household sewing.

Much of the material purchased, whether linen, cotton, or wool, came undyed in its natural tannish shades. The finer material was often sent to professional dyers in Philadelphia to be sure of a handsome result. A good deal of the dyeing, however, was done at home. Dyeing was a complicated process, and some households that did really large amounts of dyeing had a separate dye house equipped with vats and special implements. The Lewises, however, did not have such elaborate equipment.

75,76
77,79

Prior to the 1856 invention of synthetic anilene or coal tar dyes which gave brilliant and long-lasting colors, all dyes used were made from natural products, usually vegetable. They gave lovely soft shades, but it was very difficult to get dyes that were brilliant in color, that did not fade rapidly in air and sunlight, and would adhere firmly to textiles and not wash out. Madder for red and indigo for blue were two of the most effective of the natural dyes and were consequently much in demand on the world market. The other dye products called for in these recipes were the ones most commonly used by dyers though they did not compare with madder and indigo for brilliance and permanence.

Storage of the dyestuffs was extremely important so that they would retain their full strength. All the dyes would have been kept in the cellar to keep light and air from acting on them and reducing their strength.

Sticks of logwood, redwood, and sumach would be kept covered, raised off the ground. The chipped and ground woods, roots, and dried leaves and berries—logwood, madder, fustic, redwood, sumach—would be kept in covered casks. Indigo was made into a paste and kept closed tight in a box. Both cochineal and copperas were kept covered in earthenware jugs, stored in a dark place.

The process of dyeing required a vat or cauldron large enough to hold the amount of cloth to be dyed. Boiling the material was almost always part of the process; it ensured that the color would hold. As it boiled, the cloth was stirred with a long-handled dyer's rake to ensure even distribution of color without spotting. Afterward the cloth was spread over a board out of the sun to dry.

An essential ingredient in any dye recipe was the mordant. A mordant is a substance that causes the dye to bite into the fabric, that is, to adhere to the textile fibers and hold its color. Alum was one of the most commonly used because it was effective, cheap, and easily obtained. Bran was often added to the dye mixture if it was getting weak in order to extend its usefulness. It helped keep the dyestuff active.

The proper care and cleaning of clothing was a matter of great concern to the careful housewife. She had to know the proper way to wash and iron clothes even though she did not actually do the work herself. Careless washing of the natural fabrics and dyes of the period would result in shrunken and faded clothes, necessitating expensive replacements. Ordinarily, Mrs. Lewis would probably have relied on memory and not have recorded such commonplace recipes. However, she was probably preparing this book for her daughter to take into the wilds of Louisiana. Mrs. Lewis constantly worried that her daughter would be unable to find properly trained slaves in Louisiana and would be forced to take totally untrained slaves for the house and teach them basic household chores. That is probably the reason for including washing, starching, and ironing instructions. 141,143 149

Washing in those days was a major operation. It was done once a week and involved huge amounts of hot water and soap. All the family's clothes as well as table cloths, napkins, bed linens, and rags would be done. Soft water was necessary for washing to make the soap suds. Rain water in barrels or cisterns was often saved for this purpose. If there was insufficient rain water, regular water could be softened by being mixed with lye or potash.

Soap was made at home and, like slaughtering, was done once a year. The soap-making process began with lye, another homemade product with a variety of uses around the house. Lye was made from wood ash, preferably hickory or oak. Wood ash from the several hearths in the house would be scooped up and saved in a large barrel. Boiling water was poured over the ash and let stand until it was cold. The resulting liquid was then drained off and strained. Sometimes it was poured through the ash again until the desired strength of lye was obtained.

Grease from the kitchen and butchering were saved in earthen crocks or barrels throughout the year. At soap-making time the grease and lye were combined in a huge cauldron outdoors over a large hot fire. Three or four pounds of grease were added for each bucket of lye. The mixture was boiled slowly all day until it was thick and ropy, bright brown, clear, and thick as jelly. It was cooled in tubs and then stored in barrels in a dry place. When wanted, it was scooped out with a dipper. This soft soap was used for most laundry, for kitchen washing, and for a good deal of cleaning. It lasted at least a year and was used until the next year's soap-making extravaganza.

Hard soap was made the same way except that only the cleanest, clarified kitchen fat was used. It was boiled very hard with a bit of lime. After it turned to jelly, salt and other substances for special purposes, such as bayberry tallow, sand, or resin, would be added. It was allowed to cool and then melted again and placed in molds to harden.

Laundry was done in large copper or brass kettles; iron could not be used because it would stain the clothes. Besides soap, a blueing bag was used for white clothes; the blueing bag was a white flannel bag with indigo sewed inside. It was submerged in the rinse water and was squeezed to give a light blue color to the water.

Starch was a necessity on washing and ironing days as almost all whites—from petticoats to sheets—were starched. Stiff starching of shirts, collars and table linen was essential. Starch was made from various substances mixed with water, including flour, gum arabic, and glue. Salt was often added to keep colors from running. Like alum, it acted as a mordant.

Household and Hobby Products

Most of the household cleaning products were made at home even though some commercial cleaning and polishing products were on the market by the 1830s. These few recipes included by Mrs. Lewis in her collection were obviously only a random selection which did not truly reflect all the products used at Woodlawn.

The recipe for furniture polish indicates the prevailing fashion in furniture of the time. Very shiny mahogany of a dark red-brown color was considered most elegant in decorating a fine home.

18

This polish would clean and shine; the red dye would help to maintain the red color of the wood.

Broken china would clearly be a problem in a house where dinner was routinely served to large numbers of people every day with numerous maids and waiters carrying dishes back and forth to a separate kitchen; breakage must have been frequent. Very valuable pieces might have been taken to experts in town for mending, but most broken china would be mended at home. 48,151

Keeping Woodlawn clean must have been a continual occupation. With the men of the household farming, hunting, and fishing, and a large shifting population of children and guests, a lot of dirt must have been tracked in. Many cleaning and scrubbing products were used, but lime and soda were two of the standbys. They were used because of their bleaching, disinfecting, and deodorizing properties and were particularly valuable in the kitchen and basement. 156,157

Bottle cement was an important product used in preserving. After fruits, vegetables, or pickles were placed in a bottle, a cork was placed in the neck of the bottle and then covered with bottle cement to prevent air from entering and causing decomposition. 83

Honey was used in cooking and on the many hot breads, waffles, and pancakes that were served in Virginia. Although it could not compare with cane sugar in importance as a sweetener, honey was considered important enough to assure a supply through beehives in the garden. A recipe to kill a common hive pest was valuable for the household. 150

A scattering of recipes in the collection are concerned with arts and crafts — painting techniques and methods of making decorative baskets and beads. Mrs. Lewis continued her artistic activities into old age and was naturally interested in collecting such advice. 160,170 171-172

The recipe for preserving animal skins was clearly meant for the benefit of Lorenzo Lewis, whose hobby was taxidermy. The hall of Audley was filled with cases of stuffed animals and birds which he had prepared. He was particularly interested in collecting unusual specimens and wanted his sister to send him samples from Louisiana. Mrs. Lewis obviously got this recipe so that the Butlers could send skins to Virginia without spoiling. 47

—✠—

Modern Methods

It might be entertaining for the dedicated craftsman to try some of the dyeing, painting, or household product recipes, but under no circumstances whatsoever should any of the medical recipes be used. Given the state of nineteenth-century medicine, it would be sheer foolhardiness of the most dangerous kind. However, the cookery recipes are definitely usable. The following suggestions and instructions apply only to them:

The sheer enormity of some of these recipes might be frightening to many modern cooks, so that the first piece of advice is to cut and cut again. Unless cooking for an orphanage, cut the recipes in half or even a quarter for a manageable size. Modern ovens are not designed to hold a gargantuan cake made with thirty eggs.

Many of these recipes are not really complete, so watch for obvious omissions such as flour from a cake recipe. Many types of vinegar were used; either wine or cider vinegar will be appropriate in most recipes. Sea salt or kosher salt should generally be used. In cooking, regular table salt may be substituted, but it will not be effective in curing meat. Use white rice, not brown. Unflavored gelatin replaces isinglass, following package directions. Either of the common baker's yeasts may be used. Compressed yeast may be dissolved in lukewarm water or milk. Active dry yeast should be dissolved in slightly warmer water, never in milk. Use stone ground corn meal or mix equal parts white and yellow meal.

Directions are the same for whole classes of recipes. Yeast breads should be thoroughly kneaded, covered, and placed in a warm place to rise; they should be punched down and allowed to rise a second time before baking. Pans should be greased and lightly floured. Baking time will vary depending on pan size, but the bread should be brown and have a hollow sound when thumped.

Cakes need to be beaten thoroughly. Medium eggs should be used since the eggs of the period were smaller than those of today. Yolks and whites should be beaten separately before adding other ingredients. They should usually, unless the recipe directs otherwise, be creamed with sugar and butter. White granulated sugar and lightly salted butter will be acceptable.

Unbleached stone ground flour is most authentic, but all-purpose white flour may be used with good results. Flour should be sifted for any recipe. Baking soda should be substituted for potash, pearl ash, or saleratus. An equivalent amount of soda should work well. Milk was richer at the time than today, so use half and half when milk is called for and heavy whipping cream for cream.

When wine is called for, use a sweet dessert wine. Madeira or sweet sherry would be good choices. The measurement of a wine glass clearly varied a great deal. A good effect can be achieved by using two ounces of wine when a wine glass is called for and one ounce when a half wine glass is specified, although more wine may be added to taste.

Spices and flavoring ingredients should be added with a heavy hand for an authentic effect because the fashion was for highly flavored food. Powdered spices are acceptable, but freshly ground nutmeg, mace, and cinnamon will taste better. Almonds may be ground in a mortar or in a food processor. Prepared almond paste may be used, but the amount of sugar will have to be decreased correspondingly.

Rose water was the essential flavoring ingredient of the nineteenth century so it is worth the effort of finding it at a large pharmacy or gourmet food store. If unavailable, any of the common flavoring extracts—vanilla, almond, lemon, or orange—may be substituted in the proportion of one tablespoon to one wine glass of rose water, but the taste of the recipe will be altered.

Loaf cakes, not layer cakes, were the rule of the period; other than that, cakes may be baked in any shape pan desired. Fancy molds, particularly the turk's head, would be most appropriate. Pans should be greased and lightly floured. Cooking time will depend on the pan size; the cake will be done when a straw comes out clean. The great cakes may be frosted with almond or lemon icing, but most cakes should not be iced. They should be garnished with powdered sugar and served with ice cream or a sauce. Cakes will be considerably heavier and denser than most modern cakes.

Oven temperature is a difficult question as the ovens of the period were, of course, unregulated. Use of the following suggestions as a rough guideline: a brisk, hot, or fast oven calls for a high temperature, probably 375° to 400° F.; a medium oven would be 325° to 350°; and a slack or slow oven would require a very low temperature, 200° to 275° depending on how much the recipe emphasizes slow cooking for a long time.

When serving any of these dishes, remember that presentation was as important as cooking. Everything should be served in the most attractive dishes with elaborate garnishes. Let your imagination run riot with flowers, fruits, and frills.

Editorial Methods

Only those recipes actually entered by hand in the house-keeping book were considered as part of the manuscript. Newspaper clippings, whether loose or pasted in, were not transcribed. Random jottings of debts, medicine dosages, and laundry lists found in the end papers were not included. The intent in transcribing the manuscript was to reproduce it as written with as little editorial intervention as consistent with clarity. Oddities of spelling, capitalization, and punctuation were retained with the following exceptions:

1. Dashes used as terminal punctuation were replaced by periods.
2. A clearly accidental duplication of words was silently corrected.
3. Abbreviations were expanded with brackets when the meaning would have been obscure to the average reader.
4. Untitled recipes were given titles, enclosed in brackets, consistent with the style of other titles in the manuscript.
5. Numbers were assigned consecutively to each recipe by the editor to facilitate reference in the introduction.

Recipes

Recipes

Recipes

1 [To Keep Butter]

To Keep Butter Sweet through the summer season disolve saltpeter & Loaf sugar together   Brown sugar will do   prepare your butter for use as in Common & Immerse it in the Liquid & Keep it continuely coverd & it will Keep sweet & good   it has been Tryd

Wm. B. Harrison

2 To Preserve Strawberries

Strain a pint of the juice for which allow half a pound of sugar. then a pint of liquor to a pound more of sugar to a pound of Strawberries, boil the liquor with the sugar 'till it becomes almost a syrup, then throw in the strawberries, & let them boil very *fast* 'till done.

3 Flannel Cakes

1 qt of flour
3 eggs
3 large spoonfuls of yeast
1 spoonful of butter, make them up with milk rather thicker than pancake batter, bake them on a griddle greased with lard   lay them up to lighten late at night, not too warm   When you wish them for Tea make them up at 2'oclock P.M.

4 Waffles

Take the yolks of three eggs, take three large spoonfuls of flour, & a pint of new milk, beat them very light, & pour into your moulds, when one side is done, turn on the other, & bake another, on clean fine coals, send them quick to table in a napkin.

5 *Phila. Buns*

¼ lb of Flour, ½ lb of butter, the butter to be cut up in the flour, Then add a pint of milk, a little rose water, brandy & wine, half a wine glass of yeast, 4 eggs well beaten, a little cinnamon & nutmeg, a few currants, ½ lb of sugar sifted & not to be added until they have stood, take ¼ lb. of flour & work it in with a knife, & put them to rise in a greased pan.

---

6 *Eggbread*

1 pint of meal

1 pint of milk, a spoonful of butter, 1 d[itt]o. of salt, beat an Egg, mix in the milk & the meal which should have the butter previously rubbed in.

---

7 *Sponge Cake*

3 doz eggs, whites & yolks beaten separately, leave out half the whites. a light spoonful of flour, & rather more of sugar to each egg. beat them very light, add a glass of wine, the juice of 2 lemons, & the peels of 4. bake quick.

---

8 *Mrs Lee's Gingerbread*

6 lbs of flour, 2 lbs of butter rolled in very fine, 2 lbs Sugar, 2 ozs of ginger, 2 lbs or pints of molasses, half a pint of cream warmed in together with the molasses, mix well, roll thin, cut them with a cup, & bake them in a slack oven.

---

9 *Rice Pancakes*

Boil half a lb of Rice to a jelly in water, when cold mix it with a pint of cream, 8 eggs well beaten, a desert spoonful of beaten mace, cinnamon or nutmeg, stir in 8 ozs butter creamed, & as much flour as will make the batter thick enough, fry in butter, or as little lard as possible.

10 *Potatoe Fritters*

Beat the yolks of 6 eggs very light, add to them a quart of milk, boil as many Irish potatoes as will make a quart, skin & beat them very fine, put them into the milk & eggs, & thicken with flour, the thickness of common fritter batter, beat all 'till very light. fry in lard as common fritters.

11 *Baked Wine Custards*

The yolks of 9 eggs, beat them a little light, add half a pint of wine, sweeten'd to your taste, add a little beaten mace or cinnamon, put it into cups & grate nutmeg over it, & bake it   put water in the oven before you put your cups in.

12 *To Preserve Pears*

To ev'ry lb. of Pears, 1 lb. of sugar beaten & sifted, put your sugar into your preserving pan, & add as much water as will be sufficient to cover your pears, let it boil, then put in your pears, & stew them gently until they are done, & of a pretty pink color, then take out your fruit & let the syrup boil until it is as thick as you like, then pour it over the fruit & let it stand until cold.

13 *Oyster Soup*

Take 2 quarts of Oysters, drain them in a cullender, take the liquor, put it in a stew pan with a few slips of bacon, when the Bacon is done, put in the Oysters, a bunch of sweet herbs, a pint of milk, or half a pint of cream, a spoonful of butter rolled in flour, season to your taste.

14 *Cabbage Pudding*

Take a bit of stale bread & grate it, 2 or 3 slices of Bacon, also of veal or any cold meat, chop it fine, sweet herbs sliced fine, a large onion, yolks of 3 eggs, pepper & salt, of boiled cabbage a large bit chopped up with it. beat all well together, take a large Cabbage, cut a hole at the end, where the stalk was, get out all the inside, then put in the above ingredients, tie up the cabbage in a napkin, let it boil for three hours.

15 *Green Crab Apples*

Gather your apples with care, do not bruise them, those that are free from specks put into a copper Saucepan to green, as soon as they are begin to grow tender, so that the skin will peel off, take them out carefully, & take off the peels. then have ready a syrup of a pound of sugar to a pint of water, lay your apples in the syrup, & let them stand until the next day, then set them on the fire, & let them boil until they are quite transparent, take them out, & put them into a glass vessel. The Syrup must be boiled to a jelly, & when cold put it to the apples which must be cover'd with it. put 2 lbs of sugar to one pound of Apples.

---

16 *Brandy Peaches*

After paring your peaches, put them into a Saucepan, sprinkling them with a small quantity of sugar, tie the pot close & set it in an iron pot of cold water, let it boil until your peaches become tender, then separate them from the liquor & broken pieces, put them into a clean pot, spoon your sweeten'd Brandy on them. To every quart of Brandy add a pound of sugar. The liquor that comes from the Peaches with sugar & Brandy added to it makes an excellent cordial with the addition of a few peach kernels.

---

17 *Tomata Catsup*

Wash your pot very clean, put your Tomata's in it & let it stand over the fire 'till the juice is extracted, then strain it through a hair seive, add salt & spice to your taste, set it on again & boil it, scumming carefully until no scum remains, let it be perfectly cold before you bottle it, cork it tight & keep it in a cool place.

---

18 *To Polish Furniture*

1 oz of Alkanet root,
1 oz of rose pink, 1 pint cold drawn linseed oil. To give the mahogany color. 2 drachms of Dragons blood, 7 d]itt]o. Alkanet root, half a drachm of rectified spirits of wine, previous to this application stain your wood with Aqua Fortis.

from the A[merican]. Farmer

68

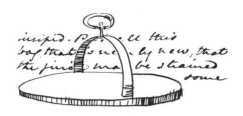

insipid. B... ll this
... that ... ... by new, that
the juice ma... be strained
some

19 Flannel Cakes

2 lbs flour, 6 eggs well beaten, 1 wine glass of yeast, a little salt, wet it with milk into a thin batter, & set it to rise, bake on a griddle.

---

20 Cocoanut Pudding

½ lb of butter, & ½ lb of sugar beat to a cream, the whites of 8 eggs well beaten, half a wine glass of brandy, wine, & rose water; & ½ lb of cocoanut grated fine, & mixed in together by degrees. This quantity will make 3 Puddings. One cocoanut is half a lb generally.

---

21 Lemon Pudding

½ lb of butter, ½ lb of Sugar beat to a cream, 5 eggs beat to a high froth, grate in the rind of 1 large lemon   squeeze in the juice, then add half a glass of brandy, wine & rose water, the 3 together to make the half glass. (2 Puddings.)

---

22 Pumpkin Pudding

½ lb of butter, ½ lb of sugar beat to a cream, 7 lb of pumpkin, stewed & passed through the cullender, 4 eggs, one wine glass of brandy wine & rose water   one teaspoonful of spice.

---

23 Potato Pudding

1 lb of butter, 1 lb of sugar, beat to a cream, 1 lb of potatoes boiled & passed through a cullender, 8 eggs, one glass of Brandy, one of wine, half a glass of rose water, one teaspoonful of spice.

24 *Orange Pudding*

1 lb of butter, 1 lb of sugar, beat to a cream, 1 glass of Brandy, wine & rose water, 10 eggs beat to a high froth, pare 2 oranges & boil the rinds 'till tender (change the water twice or 3 times) then beat in a mortar, & squeeze in the juice together with the rind of one lemon grated, & the juice of the same. For Apple Puddings add four large spoonfuls of strained apples to each pudding.

---

25 *Almond Pudding*

1/2 a lb of butter, 1/2 lb of sugar beat to a cream, 1/2 lb of Almonds blanched, & beaten very fine; beat them well together & add 5 eggs, one wine glass of brandy, wine, & rose water. 2 Puddings.

---

26 *Tomata Catsup*

Wipe the Tomata's clean & slice them in a deep pan   to every layer sprinkle a handful of salt, let them lie twelve hours, put them in a skillet & let them boil four or five minutes, then strain them through a coarse cloth, to get all the juice, pour it in the skillet again, & boil it briskly 30 minutes; to one quart of liquor add a quarter of an oz of mace, ginger & half a quarter of an oz of white pepper, strain it through a thin cloth, & when cold, bottle it, & cork it tight; put 4 or 5 blades of mace, & six cloves in each bottle, & some nutmeg. shake the bottle when used.

27 *Mrs M.L.C.'s Rolls*

1 1/2 qrts of flour at night made up, a spoonful of butter, 2 eggs & milk sufficient to make it into thin dough, with as much yeast as is usually put in the same quantity of bread. make them into rolls in the morning, & bake them in a tin pan of round shape.

28 *Recipe to Cure Hams*

Take 12 lbs of Salt. 8 gallons of water, & half lb of Salt Petre.
2 lbs of Sugar, in this proportion make enough to cover the meat;
then take a little Salt, sugar & Salt Petre. & dry rub the Hams with
them, pack them down very hard in a Cask, & pour on the Pickle
above mention'd till it covers them; let them remain in it six weeks,
then smoke them, after which hang them in a cool place to get wind
dried, put every piece in a separate coarse, thick, close, linen bag.
and keep them in a dry cool cellar.

29 *Recipe for Soft Gingerbread*

Take 3 cups of Molasses, 1 cup of Butter or drippings 2 table
spoonfuls of ginger. 3 Eggs. 1 cup of milk, 1 teaspoonful of Pearl
ash.

30 *Smoked Beef*

The Recipe for smoked Beef is the same as for the Hams,
except, that in place of 2 lb of sugar, take 2 qrts. of Molasses. The
Beef must be put in bags also.

31 *For Crullers*

Take 2 lbs of flour, 4 eggs, ³/₄ lb of sugar. & ³/₄ lb of butter &
1 tea cup of milk.

32 *For Dough Nuts*

Take 2 lbs of flour, 2 Eggs, 1 lb of sugar. 1 pint of Milk, 6
ozs of butter. some ginger & yeast, put to sponge.

33 *Recipe for Pickling Oysters*

Drain all the liquor from the Oysters, put them in scalding Salt & water, & stir them for a quarter of an hour over the Fire. then take them out & put them in cold water, after this put them in a pot. strain their own liquor & boil it. put some Alspice & cloves tyed in a Bag in the liquor, then some mace, cayenne pepper & vinegar, not tyed up. The quantities of the latter ingredients to be suited to your taste. They must be pickled 3 days before they are used.

34 *Stewed Beef. Mrs. Barry*

A Rump of Beef—take the bone out, then roll & bind it with broad tape very close, put it in a cloth, & then in a vessel with a sufficiency of water to cover it, let it stew gently till done. Then melt about an oz of butter in a sauce pan, When boiling, put in flour gently until it is brown & thick, mix about a pint of boiling water, it should be smooth, strain it thro' a sieve, & put as much of it in the drawn gravy (made as hereafter mention'd) as will thicken it sufficiently. a little mace, cloves, pepper, then put it on a slow fire & let it boil, after strain it through a sieve. then chop very fine a few pickled cucumbers, 6 onions, & a few capers.

35 *To Make Rich Soup*

A shin or any other lean piece of Beef put on a slow fire cover'd with water, put in a bunch of Thyme, a bunch of parsley, a little celery, 2 onions stuck with a few cloves, let them boil all night, then Strain it through a sieve & let it cool so as to get into a jelly, then mix a little of the drawn gravy into it, (if made sufficiently strong it will not require the gravy.) have ready to throw into your soup, carrots cut in slices & notched at the edges, turnips about an inch long & fluted—the cuts taken out also, all boiled in a saucepan separately in water, strained & put into the soup. Catsup & seasoning to your taste.

36 Hansons Mode of Making Chicken Broth; the Best in the World

Take a large chicken, kill, scald, pick, clean, & skin it. put it into a pot with a close cover   pour in 3 pints of cold water, let it simmer slowly. in half an hour put in a little Thyme. half an hour after, a tablespoonful of flour & water mixed smooth & stirred in When the bones come thro' the meat, it is done. It must never boil, only simmer slowly. If a small chicken, 1 quart of water is enough. If you wish it very nourishing—break the bones with a rolling pin before you put it into the pot. Chicken water is the best remedy for Cholera Morbus. first, warm water or weak chamomile tea, then chicken water. So tho't Dr. Jenifer who was celebrated for the cure of that disease.

---

37 Pepper Gargle for Sore Throats

2 large Pods of red pepper   pour on them a quart of boiling water   let it stand cover'd close until it burns the mouth pretty well, then put it into a bottle   add 2 tablespoons of vinegar & one of honey. gargle frequently, & swallow a little occasionally—a few drops each time of gargling. Cayenne pepper will do as well as pods   2 heap'd teaspoonsful to a quart of water.

---

38 Paste

1 lb butter, 1 lb flour, work it very little, roll in the butter four times. roll it out cut & bake it.

---

39 Bun Cakes

1 ½ pints of flour, 4 eggs, 1 table spoon of butter, small cup of sugar, 4 table spoons of strong yeast; make up with milk, set to rise at night   in the morning work in a little flour, set it to rise in the baking pan, then bake it slowly.

40 *Yeast*

Boil a quarter of a pound of hops in two gallons soft water. when boiled half an hour—strain and add one table-spoonful of salt. half a pint of molasses. two quarts of rye-meal. half a pint good common yeast. let it stand till it ferments. then stir in Indian meal till it is as hard and stiff as can be made, then roll it to the thickness of half an inch. cut it into pieces of 2- or 3- inches diameter, lay it on a board to dry—in the sun or a warm room. When quite dry it will keep excellent for six months.

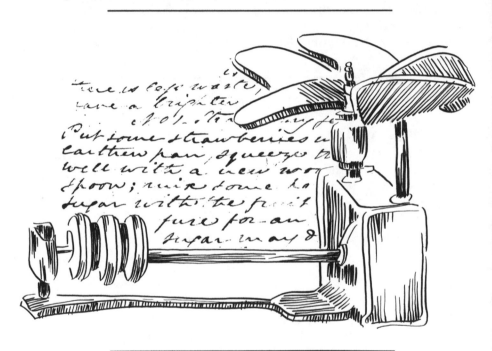

41 *Tomato Soup*

Take 6 large onions, fry them in a quarter of a pound of butter, toast six large slices of bread quite brown & hard, & take care not to burn them. take about 20 Tomata's, slice them & wash them clean & take out every seed. put all the above materials in a clean pot that will hold one gallon & fill it with boiling water. season it high with pepper & salt & let it stew gently 'till it is rich, stir it often, when you are ready to dish it, pass it through a cullender into a Tureen upon fried bread cut dice fashion. —If the Tomata's are small it will require a double quantity.

42 *Recipe for India Pickle*

Take 1 pound of ginger, lay it in salt & water one night, scrape & slice it thin, then put it into a Bottle with dry salt till the other ingredients are ready. peel & slice 1 lb of Garlick, salt it for three days, wash & salt it 3 days longer. then wash & dry it in the Sun. put a lb of long pepper in salt & water for one night, take it out   clean salt & dry it   1 lb of horseradish, wash, scrape, & slice it thin, then salt & dry it. Take 2 ozs of Turmerice beat fine, half a lb strongest mustard seed beat fine, put into a stone jar, & pour on them 1 gallon strong vinegar, place the jar in a cool dry place & put on it an Iron cover. do not tie it down, or boil the vinegar. let this stand shaking it well every day for 2 or 3 weeks, then put in vegetables as they come in season, prepared in this way—cut cabbages & cauliflowers in quarters, take young corn, young onions, young asparagus, beans &c. lay them in a brine of salt & vinegar 3 weeks. take them out, dry them part of two days. then wash them in vinegar, squeeze & put them into your pot   tie a thick paper over it or a linen & bladder. It is not to be eaten for six months. add vinegar &c if the quantity is not sufficient—or make double the quantity at once. for a 3 gallon pot. Asparagus should be scalded first.

---

43 *Mrs C Carters Gingerbread. Excellent*

To a quart of flour add half a pound of butter, The yolks of 3 eggs, a small plate of brown sugar, six spoonfuls of powder'd ginger, & molasses enough to wet it up, say nearly a pint. Then bake it on tin or Iron plates.

---

44 *To Preserve Tomata's during Winter*

Peel your Tomata's, cut them small & stew them in their own juice, season with salt, pepper, grated ginger, garlick pounded fine, to your taste, when cool put it in bottles cork & wax them, examine them frequently, if you observe any effervescence or a disposition to ferment heat them over the fire. They must be done in an earthen pan to retain the fine red color. They require to be kept on the fire some considerable time, until some are wasted or they will not keep.

45 *Plum Pudding*

6 ozs suet chopped fine
6 ozs Raisins stoned
8 ozs currants nicely washed
3 ozs Bread crumbs, grated
3 ozs fine flour
3 eggs
Sixth of a nutmeg
small blade of mace
same quantity of cinnamon pounded fine as possible
half a teaspoon of salt
half a pint of milk, or less
4 ozs sugar
1 oz candied lemon peel sliced
1/2 oz citron sliced

Beat the eggs & spice well together, mix the milk with them by degrees, then the rest of the ingredients, dip a fine close linen cloth into boiling water, & put it in a hair sieve flour it a little, put in the Ingredients   tie it up close; put it into a saucepan containing six quarts of water, boiling, keep a kettle of boiling water alongside of it, & fill up your pot as it wastes; be sure to keep it boiling six hours at least.

46 *My Pudding*

Beat up the yolks & whites of 3 eggs, strain them thro' a sieve & gradually add to them about a quarter pint of milk, stir them well together. rub together in a mortar 2 ozs moist sugar, & as much grated nutmeg as will be on a sixpence.

47 *To Dress Skins with the Fur On*

Wash them quite clean of flesh & then wash them in soap & water. then lay them in a strong solution of Allum. wring them as dry as possible & rub the skin side quite dry with pounded Allum. A large skin may be allowed to soak from six to twelve hours & a shorter time for small, or Hare skins.

48 *[To Mend China]*

Beat up the whites of fresh eggs; add to it as much fine quick lime as will give it a tolerable consistence, apply it to the broken pieces of China and join them together. after they are dry, boil them in milk—& the seam will not be so visible. Should they come apart—from boiling—the operation may be performed again.

49 *Raspberry Vinegar*

To a quart of Raspberries—add a quart of vinegar. let them stand 24 hours. strain the Raspberries through a sifter and add a quart of fresh raspberries to the same vinegar. let it stand another 24 hours. again strain off the liquor and add a quart of fresh Raspberries. let these also stand 24 hours. Then strain off the liquor and add to each pint of the liquor 12 oz. of white sugar. stew it half an hour in your preserving pan. taking off the scum as it rises.

50 *Peach Liquer*

Fill your cask with peaches nicely pared. then fill it with peach brandy. adding to every gallon of brandy 1 lb of brown sugar. let it stand three months. then drain off the liquor in demijohns and fill your cask with boiling water. let that stand three weeks. draw off the liquor adding to every gallon a pound of sugar. then mix the first and second draining together. put in with your first brandy some orange peel.

51 *Recipes for Cakes—Wonders*

2 lbs flour
3/4 lb of sugar
1/2 lb butter, 9 eggs, a little mace & rosewater.

52 *Pound Cake*

9 eggs, 3 spoonsful butter
3 spoonfuls of sugar, 3 handfuls of flour.

53 *Cream Cake*

4 teacups, flour. 3 of sugar, 1 of butter, 1 of cream, 5 eggs, 1 teaspoon of pearl ash, first rub the butter & sugar together, then add the rest.

54 *Composition Cake*

1 lb of flour, 1 of sugar, half pound of butter, 7 eggs, half pint of cream, gill of french Brandy.

55 *Jumbles*

3 lbs flour, 2 of sugar, 1 of butter
8 eggs, a few carraway seeds,
& a little milk if the eggs are not sufficient.

56 *Love Cake*

1 & ½ lbs of butter rubbed into 2 lbs of flour, 1 egg, 1 glass of wine, 1 wine glass of rose water, 2 of yeast, & a small quantity of nutmeg, cinnamon & currants, baked in little pans.

57 *Tea Cakes*

3 tea cups of sugar, 3 eggs, 1 tea cup butter, 1 of milk, a small lump of pearl ash, to be made not quite so stiff as pound cake.

58 *Sponge Cake*

5 eggs, half pound sugar, 1 lb of flour, & a little cinnamon.

59 *Cookies*

1 tea cup of butter, 1 of sugar, 1 egg & some flour.

60 Matrimony Cakes

1 pint of dough, 1 cup of sugar
1 cup of butter, 3 eggs,
1 tea spoon of pearl ash, with raisins & spices.

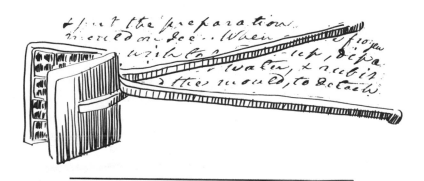

61 Wafers

1 lb of flour, ¼ lb butter, 2 eggs beaten, 1 glass of wine & a nutmeg.

62 Clove Cake

3 lbs of flour, 1 lb butter, 1 of sugar, 3 eggs, 2 spoonsful cloves, mix it with molasses.

63 Courtship Cake

5 lbs of flour, 2 of sugar, ¾ of Lard, ¾ of butter, 1 pint of yeast, 8 eggs, 1 quart of milk, roll the sugar in the flour, add raisins & spice after the first rising.

64 An Indian Pudding

3 pints of scalded milk, 7 spoonfuls of fine Indian meal, mix well together while hot, let it stand until cool, then add 4 eggs, half pound butter, some spices, & sugar   let it bake four hours.

65 *Recipe for Lip Salve*

Take of Virgin Wax . . . . .2 oz
            Hog's Lard. . . . . .2 oz
            Sperma Ceti . . . . .1/2 oz
            Oil of Almonds . . . . .1 oz
            Balsam Peru . . . . .2 drms.
            Alkanet Root. . . . . .2 drms.
            New Raisins (Shred Small) No 6
            White Sugar in Powder . . . . .¹/₂ drm.

Simmer them all together a little while. then Strain
We add 2 drms. of Ess. Lemon to give the lipsalve a fine odour.

E.S.

---

66 *[For Lumps or Swelling in the Breast]*

For Lumps, or Swelling in the breast, nothing is so good as
the white of raw eggs. spread on linen. and applied wet to the place.
it must be frequently moistened in the egg.

---

67 *Black Cake. Mrs L's*

30 eggs, yolks & whites beaten seperately, cream 3 lbs butter, add the whites by degrees, then pound & sift 3 lbs fine sugar &
add to the butter & whites. then the yolks then 3 ¹/₂ lbs flour, dried
& sifted. 8 nutmegs & a large handful of mace beaten fine, preserved
orange peel or dried orange a double handful, pounded fine. 4 ¹/₂ lbs
dried currants 4¹/₂ lbs raisins cut & stoned
            preserved ginger beaten fine, & sliced citron improvements.
3 quarters of a pint, or a large tumbler & a half of french
brandy. mix all well together & bake slowly. & well.

---

68 *Sponge Cake*

10 eggs, the weight in sugar half the weight in flour. beat
whites & yolks seperately   mix them together & grate the rinds of 2
lemons, add the ingredients, flour & sugar, by spoonfuls alternately
until it is all mixed. bake quick, set it on end (when done) to cool.

69 *Mrs P's Sponge Cake*

12 eggs, their weight in sugar, weight of 7 in flour. 12 yolks , 9 whites beat seperately 'till light, then mix yolks & whites sugar & flour, rinds of 3 lemons, juice of one. beat all well together, bake in a large pan or small ones, sift fine sugar over, bake in a quick oven.

70 *Recipe for Chapped Hands*

Sassafras root sliced & stewed in Lard or cream, to a salve.

71 *Lap-land Cakes*

Take 2 quarts of flour. A spoonfull of butter. two Eggs, A small Cup of good brisk yeast, mix it up well with warm milk, not so stiff as bread it must be very well worked when made up at night & worked up early in the morning to lay to lighten; before it is put into the Oven—to be made in little Cakes half an inch thick.

72 *To Preserve Eggs*

Put a pint of Lime to every Gallon of water till all are Coverd.

73 *Blackberry Cordial*

Take a clean Keg, fill it as full as possible with very ripe blackberries fill up with old Whiskey, let it stand 3 months shaking it up occasionally, then draw off all the liquid, put it into a Vessel & stop it tight, then fill the cask again with soft water, draw that off, then add to the water drawn off, 3 lbs of sugar for every gallon of water & spirit, throw in a little cloves or alspice boil it until clarified, & pour it boiling into the spirit. The older it is the better. Damson, cherry or currant or peach cordial are made in the same way, but to the peach & currant you put nutmeg & mace instead of cloves & alspice. green grapes of any kind boiled & prepared in the same way make a delicious cordial. to all light color'd fruits, nutmeg & mace.

74 *Brandy Peaches*

Put your peaches in boiling ley [lye] strong enough to bear an Egg, take them out immediately & throw them in cold water. make a thick syrup & let them simmer in it a few minutes, then put them in a jar & cover them with Brandy   leave them 24 hours, pour off the brandy & mix an equal quantity of syrup with it. to make the syrup, ½ lb of sugar to 1 lb of Peaches.

---

75 *Dyes—for Black*

For 20 lbs of clean scour'd woollen, 3 lbs chipped or ground Logwood, boil together for 2 ½ hours Take it out of the liquor cool it for 20 or 30 minutes, then add to the liquor 2 ½ lbs Copperas & boil it gently for 2 hours or more & you will have a good black. as much water as necessary to cover the woollen put to the 3 lbs Logwood.

---

76 *For Red*

20 lbs clean scour'd woollen   3 lbs of Alum, boil gently in as much water as will cover it 2 ½ hours, take out & wash clean, then take 6 lbs good madder a quart of bran & get soft water   add to your Alum water cold, & bring it up to a good *Scald* & you will have a good red. preparation for yellow & green the same.

---

77 *Pale Blue*

Take of ground float Spanish Indigo 1 ¼ lbs. oil of vitriol 1 lb, mix them well together   add a little Salt to make it fermented. this forms a paste which keeps for years. when you wish to dye, take a copper or brass kettle full of boiling water with a little Alum in it—& add a little of your paste until the color suits your taste. it dyes silk or wool in 5 minutes or less if you wish it light. when you wish a beautiful green, boil fustic chips for an hour, add Alum & add a little of your blue paste. without the blue you have a beautiful yellow. for pink dye, use cochineal as you do fustic for yellow.

—*⊷*—

78 *To Make Alum Baskets*

Take about 4 lbs of Allum & 1 table spoonful of Gum Arabick, & dissolve them in 1 gallon of water. Let it stand half an hour to cool after straining it & then suspend the basket in it for about 16 hours. Do not allow it to touch the sides or lower part of the vessel. Cover the cane with old Muslin as, new will not attract the Allum as well.

---

79 *Ann Bambers Black Dye*

Take 1 pound of Log-wood. 1/4th lb of Redwood. or Sumach. 1/4 lb of fustic. soak them in water all night. then—put them into a ten gallon Kettle full of water. boil your silk or worsted materials three hours—in the mixture. then take them out. cool and air them. then add to your dye 1 table spoonful of coperas. let it remain until the coperas is entirely dissolved. then put in your cloths again, taking care that they are well covered by the dye. boil them for three hours more. and let them remain in the dye all night. take them out next morning. wash them out in cold water. dry and Iron them. Spots will be removed by soaking them in vinegar. Blue Black requires only Log-wood and Coperas. the dye once finished is only of use for dipping black *cloths* over again. nothing can be dyed in it.

---

80 *To Make 20 Oil Mangoes*

Take half a pound of Race Ginger, soak it in Salt & water until soft. Horse radish scraped & soaked 12 hours—half a lb. Garlic & mustard seed each half a pound soaked & dried. Clear your 20 melons of the seed, fill them with Salt, let them lie 3 day's packed close in a Colander, & cover'd with Salt. On the 4th day, wipe them very dry, The above mentioned ingredients, adding one by one of whole black pepper, salted & dried, of mace, cloves, & Turmeric each half an ounce, beat them to a paste with two table spoonfuls of sweet oil or fresh butter from the churn, fill your melons with this & put them in a stone jar, if any ingredients remain, put them in with half a pint of fresh made mustard. fill the jar with boiling vinegar. They will be fit to use in 6 months. M L C's recipe.

81 *Fox Grapes*

Take an equal weight of Fox Grapes & sugar, & moisten the sugar with water. then stew them together & if the syrup is not thick enough, separate the grapes from it, boil it again. spoon it hot over the Grapes.

---

82 *Rice Bread*

Boil a quarter of a pound of Rice (well washed) 'till it is quite soft; then put it on the back part of a seive to drain it, & when it is cold mix it with ³/₄ of a pound of flour, a tea cup of yeast, a tea cup of milk, & a small table spoonful of Salt. Let it stand for 3 hours; then knead it up, & roll it in a handful of flour, so as to make the outside dry enough to put into the oven. about an hour & a quarter will bake it, & it will produce one pound fourteen ounces of very good white bread. It should not be eaten until two days old.

---

83 *Bottle Cement*

¹/₂ lb black resin
¹/₂ lb red sealing wax
¹/₄ oz bees wax

melt in an earthen or iron pot   when it froths up before all is melted & likely to boil over stir it with a tallow candle which will settle the froth till it is melted & fit for use. This is of great use in stopping bottles well. cover the corks with it.

---

84 *Mrs. Coxe's Recipe for Green Peppers*

Put them in a strong salt & water until they are yellow, then put them on the fire in vinegar & water (half & half) until green. great care is necessary to prevent the water getting *more* than blood heat, *that it is* which makes them grow soft. as soon as they are green, boil some very strong vinegar & pour on them
stuff some if you like after greening.
a few cloves, alspice, mustard seed, horse radish & garlick as usual in green pickles.

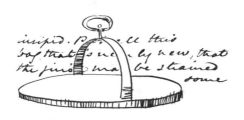

85 *Hanson's Thin Biscuits*

To one quart of flour half a pint of sweet milk one table
spoonful of Butter; mix the butter with half the flour, then work in
the milk with the flour & butter by degrees, then work in the rest of
the flour very well, make the dough stiff. then roll it hard with the
rolling pin 8 or 10 times thin, cut it out with a round tin cutter or
tumbler, stick a few holes in each biscuit with a fork, bake in an
oven not too hot, slowly; when they break *short*, & you can snap
them in half without *bending* they are done.

86 *Bread*

Take 4 ½ pints of flour, to one half of this add half a pint of
yeast & as much milk warm water as will make a stiff batter. It must
be made in a large stone pot, & cover'd with a linen cloth. as the
cold weather may make necessary add one or two blankets to the
linen cover, pressed close around the pot & keep it near a moderate
fire. at day light add the other half of the flour work it in very well,
put the dough into pieces of the size you want to bake, set them to
rise until ready to bake, put them into tin pans dredged with flour
or, if for rolls, put them close together & one in the centre, in a skillet or pan or small dutch oven, fill almost to the top of your pans
with the dough set them in a warm place, it will soon rise above the
pans. Bake in a moderate oven to give time for soaking well.

87 *Hansons Breakfast Biscuits*

Take a quart of dough, add butter the size of a hens egg,
work it up very well so as to mix the butter & dough well, roll it out
3 or 4 times cut it in small pieces, roll them up like an Egg. just
flatten them a little with the rolling pin, set them by a few minutes
to rise, & bake them in a slow oven.

88 *Mrs Clements Recipe for Brandy Peaches*

30 fine peaches not too ripe, wipe the down well from them with a wet cloth, pierce each peach with a needle, put them in boiling water until they begin to be soft. take them out, & put them into cold water. to 30 peaches take 3 lbs of fine sugar. wet it & make it a highly clarified syrup. When your peaches are cold put them into it. let them have two or three boils. take them out, let them cool & put them into glass jars. then add to your syrup as much peach Brandy as will cover them well & pour it on. tie up your glasses.

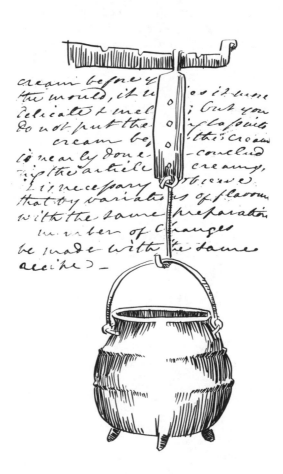

89 *To Preserve Green Figs*

Cut them in half or a third   slice from the broad end. Scrape
the pulp out carefully, then keep them in strong salt & water until
they become yellow. then wash them in fair water, prepare your
preserving pan with 3 layers of grape leaves   lay your figs on them,
cover very thick with grape leaves; lay over them cabbage leaves,
fill the pan with water & keep it just scalding hot until they are
green. do not suffer the water to boil, or even to simmer. When
green, take them out, lay them in a china or stone vessel, cover
them with cold water, change it night & morning for two days.
then make a very weak syrup, merely sweet water, boil them gently
until you can pass a straw through them. then make a rich syrup,
1½ lbs of best white sugar to one pound of Figs, & 1 pint of water,
ginger scalded & scraped to season it well, & plenty of orange citron
& lemon peels, (prepard by boiling in water until the white tough
part can be scraped out, but not too much boiled, lest they lose too
much of the strong flavour). boil fast until the syrup is rich & well
done, when it *feathers* a little as the last drops fall from the spoon, &
you observe a slight *skim* of sugar on the surface of your syrup. The
scum taken off as it rises. When done, pour them into a large bowl
until the next day. then put them into china or Queens ware, cover
with double paper (*dry* white paper next the Figs) & tie up very
closely. Citron melons or small green musk melons must be cut in
slices & done exactly in the same way, except adding *2* lbs of sugar
to each pound of rinds, with a pint & one fourth of a pint of water to
each 2 lbs of sugar. It is necessary to have more of the syrup than the
weight of the fruit requires, in order to have enough syrup to cover
them—say 4 lbs more of sugar & 2 ½ pints of water in addition to
the exact wt required for your rinds. it is necessary also for the figs
to have 3 lbs of sugar & 2 pints of water or 2 ½ pints above the exact
wt. you may put up your peels with rinds & figs if you please, but
only a *very* small part & that only the nicest small soft pieces of ginger. N.B. The boiling in thick syrup is done the *day after* the boiling
in *thin syrup or sweet water*. they remain in that all night in a large
bowl, & must be well washed in clean fresh water, *scraped* or *trimmed*
if discoloured, before you put them in the sugar & water, scraped
ginger, & peels for the thick syrup. They must all go in to the pan
together that they may heat by degrees. If you put rinds or figs into
hot syrup you will shrivel them. When they are a year old, or more,
if they are dry & too much candied to look well, pour boiling water
over them, & then make some syrup as above, & when half done,
throw in the old Figs or rinds, they will look as well as at first after
being well boiled for a short time.

90 Rinds of Ripe Water Melons

Scrape off the thin green rind but do not break the rind under it, if you can avoid it. cut out the soft pulp & let the pieces be ⅓ of an inch thick, in any shape you prefer. lay them in weak salt & water one night, the next day boil them in a great deal of water with some race ginger until a straw will pass thro' them   then wash them well in fair water, preserve them as you do Figs. viz 1 ½ lbs of Sugar, 1 pint of water to a pound of rinds. scrape ginger & peels as for the figs. put them in pots the next day.

91 Cream of Rice

This is flour of rice, which you make in the following manner. Take a pound of rice well washed in different waters & drained & wiped with a clean towel. Let it get quite dry; then pound & shake it through a sieve. Take one or two spoonfuls of this flour, & dilute it with broth, rather cold than hot. All this time you have some broth on the fire; throw the flour of rice thus diluted into the broth, & keep stirring it 'till you find the soup is not too thick & may boil without the rice burning.

92 German Cabbage Soup

Take a white cabbage, minced & wash it well, & let it sweat on a slow fire in a little butter. When it begins to get tender & to be a little reduced, moisten it with half broth & half gravy of veal very clear; skim off the fat, & when the soup gets of a fine brown colour, throw in slices of bread cut to the size of a penny, & send up.

93 Turnip Broth

Take about a dozen turnips, peeled & cut into slices. blanch them for a short time in water; drain them, put them with a knuckle of veal, a small piece of Beef, & the half of a hen, into a stew pan. pour some rich boiling broth over them. let the whole stew about two hours. then strain through a silk sieve.

⌐⫠⌐

94 *No. 6. Cressi or Vegetable Soup*

Take the red part of 8 carrots, 2 turnips, the white of 4 leeks.
2 onions, 3 heads of Celery, all washed very clean. mince the whole
small, put a bit of fresh butter at the bottom of stew pan, & the roots
over it; put it on a low fire. Let it sweat a long while, & stir it frequently; when fried enough to be rubbed through a tammy, add a
small crust of bread, moistened with some broth; let the whole boil
gently. When done, skim all the fat off, & rub the whole through a
Tammy. put it to boil on the corner of the stove in order to skim off
all the grease & the oil of the vegetables; then cut some crumbs of
bread into dice, fry it in butter 'till of a good colour, & put it into the
soup when you serve up. This purée may be used with rice, vermicelli, Italian paste, small macaroni.

95 *Soupe a la Condé*

Take about a pint of red beans well washed; let them soak in
soft water for about a couple of hours: then put them into a small
pan with a pound of the breast part of bacon, a knuckle of veal, &
the leg & back of a roasted fowl, if you have any such thing by you.
put the whole together with an onion stuck with 2 cloves, a carrot &
a couple of leeks, a bunch of parsley, green onions, thyme, & a little
salt & pepper. Moisten with soft cold water, & let the beans boil 'till
they are quite soft. Then take the beans, pound them, & rub them
through a sieve; moisten with the liquor sufficiently thin to admit
the fat being skimmed off. Then boil the soup in the corner of the
stove 'till all the white scum is entirely gone, then the soup must be
very red. Slices of bread fry & prepare as in No 6. The knuckle of a
ham is better than the breast of bacon—the fat is better.

96 *Purée of Green Peas*

3 pints of large peas of a nice green color, sweat them with a quarter of a pound of butter, & a handful of Parsley & green onions over a slow fire, till they be thoroughly stewed. then put them in a mortar with the parsley & green onions; when they are well pounded, rub them through a sieve & moisten this purée with the best consommé.★ leave it on the corner of the stove; for if it were to boil, the peas would lose their green color. just at the moment of sending up, put in square slices of bread nicely fried.

★consommé. Put into a stock pot, a large piece of buttock of Beef, or other part with a knuckle of veal, & the trimming of meat or fowls, according to the sauce you may wish to make. This broth will admit all sorts of veal or poultry. let the meat stew on a gentle fire. moisten with about two large ladles full of the first broth; put no vegetables into this broth except a bunch of parsley & green onions. Let them sweat thoroughly; then thrust your knife into the meat: if no blood issue, it is a sign that it is heated through. Then moisten it with boiling broth to the top, & let it boil gently for about four hours; after which use this consommé to make the sauces, or the consommé of either poultry or game. Take off the fat & scum of all the various broths, & keep the pots full, in order that the broth be not too high in color. When the broth remains too long on the fire, it loses its flavour, acquires too brown a color, & tastes strong & disagreeable.

---

97 *1st Broth*

Take part of a breast or of a rump of Beef with some of trimmings, put the meat into a pot with cold water. Set it on the fire & watch the proper moment to skim it well. If this broth is not clear & bright, the other broths & sauces will also be spoiled. Be particular in taking off the black scum; pour a little cold water into the above, to raise up the white scum. When all the scum has been removed, put in a few carrots, turnips, heads of celery, & leeks, 4 large onions, one of which is to be stuck with 5 cloves; then throw a handful of salt into the pot & let the whole simmer for five hours. Skim away all the fat & strain the broth thro a double silk sieve. Lay the piece of Beef in a braziere pan; pour over some of the Broth, to keep it hot, till the moment that you serve up. you make your broth in this manner, when you want to use the Beef for one of your removes; otherwise you cut your Beef smaller to be sooner done. This first broth serves to make all the other Broths.

98 *Jelly of Aspic for Moulds Covering Meats, Boned Fowls &c to be Made Stiff*

Put a knuckle of veal in a small pot, a small part of a knuckle of ham, some trimmings of fowl or game. Season this with onions, carrots, a bunch of herbs well seasoned; pour into it half a bottle of white wine, & moisten with good broth; let it boil gently for 4 hours, then skim away all the fat, drain it thro a silk sieve; put it in a stew pan, with two spoonfuls of Tarragon vinegar, & 4 whites of Eggs, salt & pepper to clarify; & keep stirring on the fire 'till the whole becomes very white, then put this on the side of the stove. with a little fire over the cover; when you find it clear, drain it in a cloth or jelly bag, & use it for aspic.

---

99 *Jelée of Meat for Pies*

This is not to be prepared in the same manner as the aspic. neither aromatic herbs or vinegar are to be used. The jelly is made as follows: Put into a stew pan a good piece of Beef, 2 calves feet, a knuckle of veal, remnants of fowls, or game, according to the contents of your pies, 2 onions stuck with cloves, 2 carrots, 2 shalots, a bunch of parseley & green onions, some thyme, spices, & a small piece of Ham sweat the whole over a very slow fire, then moisten with some good broth, let the stew pan be cover'd close, those ingredients stew for 4 hours, but very gently. When done, taste & season it well, & clarify as you do the aspic. in order that it may keep the better, put it into Ice.

---

100 *To Thicken Sauces. White Roux*

Put a good lump of butter into a stew pan, let it melt over a slow fire; when melted, drain the butter, & squeeze out the butter milk, then powder it over with flour, enough to make a thin paste; keep it on the fire for a quarter of an hour, take care not to let it colour, & pour it into an earthen pan to use when wanted.

101 *Brown Roux*

Put into a stew pan a piece of butter proportionate to the quantity of roux you want to prepare. Melt it gently, squeeze out the butter milk, then put flour enough to make a paste; you must fry it on a slow fire, & then put it again over very red ashes, 'till it be of a nice colour; but mind this is to be obtained only by slow degrees. When of a light brown, you pour it into an earthen pan, & keep it for use. It keeps a long time.

102 *Gravy of Veal*

Put a few slices of ham, the lean only into a pretty thick stew pan. Lay over them some fleshy pieces of veal. pour into your stew pan a sufficient quantity of first consomme to cover about half the thickness of the meat. let it sweat on the stove, over a brisk fire. Watch the stew pan & contents, for fear of burning. When the broth is reduced, thrust a knife into the meat, that all the gravy may run out; then stew the glaze more gently. let it stew 'till brown, but take care it does not burn, to prevent which put it on red hot *ashes*. Keep stirring your stew pan over the fire, in order that it may be all of the same colour. Turn the meat upside down that it may not stick. When the glaze is of a dark red colour, moisten with some hot broth; let the glaze detach before you put the stew pan on the fire or it might yet burn. season with a bunch of parsley & green onions. When the gravy has boiled for an hour, it is done enough. Take off the fat & strain it through a silken sieve.

103 *Beef Gravy*

put the Ham in slices, & slices of Beef into your pot. cut 4 large onions in halves, lay the flat parts over the Beef & ham. moisten with the first broth only. Let this sweat, in order to get all the gravy out of the beef, & when the broth is reduced, thrust a knife into the meat; let it stew gently on a slow fire 'till the gravy be of a light brown colour. Next moisten with some of the first Broth, throw in a large bunch of Parsley & of green onions, a little salt & a pepper corn. let the whole boil for one hour, take the fat off, & drain it through a silk sieve, to use it when wanted. To the bunch or bundle of parsley & green onions when you wish high seasoning, you must add 2 bunches of thyme, a bit of sweet basil, 2 cloves, & 6 leaves of mace.

104 *Le Bouillon de Sante*

Put into a pot six pounds of Beef, one half of a hen, & a knuckle of veal. Moisten with cold water. let it boil so that the scum rises by degrees; skim it well that it may be quite clear & limpid. when skimmed throw into it 2 carrots, 2 leeks & a head of Celery, 2 onions stuck with 3 cloves, & 3 turnips. Let the whole simmer gently for 4 hours. Then put a little Salt to it, & skim off the grease or fat before you use it.

105 *Macaroni with Consommé*

Take a quarter of a pound of Naples macaroni, & boil it in water until it is nearly done. Strain well, & put it into a rich consommé to boil. Let it be well done; rasp some Parmesan cheese which send up separately in a plate.

106 *Vermicelli Soup*

For 8 people take a quarter of a pound of Vermicelli, which blanch in boiling water to take off the taste of dust. Strain it & throw it into some broth that is boiling, otherwise the vermicelli would stick together, & could not be diluted unless crumbled into a thousand pieces. All pureés used as above. Mind, the Vermicelli must be boiled in broth before you mix it with any of the pureé & take care to break the vermicelli before you blanch it in the water, otherwise it will be in long pieces & unpleasant to send up. N.B. The *cressi* soup, or any kind of vegetable Purées are used for this & Rice soups. they are not made so thick for soups as for sauces.

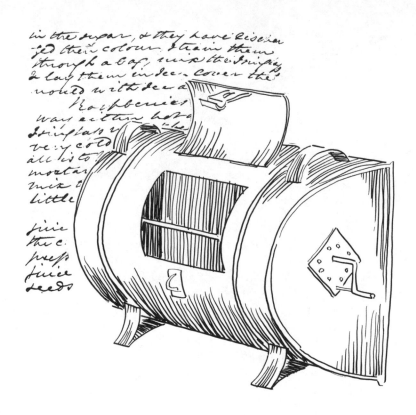

---

107 *For Rice Soup*

take half a quarter of a pound of best Rice picked clean &
washed till no smell or dirt remain. blanch it in boiling water, &
drain it. Then take some rich broth, season it well, throw the rice in
& let it boil, but not so as to be too much done, for then it breaks &
does not look well.—When to be used with different Purées mix
them together an hour before serving up that the rice may retain the
taste & colour of the vegetables.—Those most generally used with
rice are the cressi soup. carrots, turnips, celery, white beans, red
ditto, lentils, green peas The mode of proceeding is the same with
all the different kinds of pureés, They only differ in the taste & color
of the particular vegetable used. When all are mixed together they
take the name of cressi. When separate, each retains its own respec-
tive appellation, & made as the cressi.

108 *Biscuits of Potatoes*

Take 15 fresh Eggs, break the yolks into one pan, the whites in another. beat the yolks with a pound of sugar pounded very fine, scrape the peel of a lemon with a lump of sugar, dry that & pound it fine also, then throw it into the yolks, & work the Eggs & sugar until they are of a whitish colour. Next, whip the whites well; & mix them with the yolks. sift half a pound of flour of Potatoes through a silk sieve over the Eggs & sugar. Have some paper cases ready, lay on a tin with paper underneath. fill the cases, not too full glaze the contents with some sugar, which must not be pounded too fine, & bake the whole in an oven moderately heated With this quantity you may make one good cake & 24 cases. The biscuit in the mould is made with the same paste, but you put some melted butter in a mould of the shape you fancy; then take some very dry, fine white sugar & after having spread the butter all over the inside, throw the pounded sugar into it, & turn the mould all over to equalize the sugar; throw a few cinders on a baking dish, & put the mould over them to prevent its burning in the oven; put the paste gently into it, take care not to fill the mould too full, & bake it in an oven of a moderate heat. It should be of good colour. Take it out of the mould as soon as you bring it from the oven. one hour will suffice to bake it thoroughly. The flour of Potatoes is made by first peeling some raw potatoes, & then rasping them into a great vessel of clean cold water. When the Potatoes have produced a sediment at the bottom of the pan drain off all the water gently, & fill the pan again with very clean water, then stir up the sediment; & let it settle again. When settled drain off all the water, & put the sediment on a clean cloth till it is quite dry. keep it in a close pot for use.

---

109 *Omelette Soufflé*

Break six Eggs, put the whites into one pan, & the yolks into another, rasp a little lemon peel beat the yolks well, add a little sugar & salt. next beat the whites well like snow, & mix them with the yolks lightly. Then put a lump of butter into an omelette pan on the fire; when the butter is melted, pour the omelette into the pan, when it is firm enough on one side to hold the liquid part, turn it over on the dish you send up, then bake it in an oven, or use the dutch oven. When it is well raised, glaze it & send it up immediately, for it would soon lower. Mind it must be cover'd hermetically with a large fire over it, otherwise it will not rise. To this you may give whatever flavour you think proper; but the plainer the better, when served very hot, & very high.

95

110 *French Pancakes*

Put into a basin, 2 ozs of fine flour, 3 ozs of sugar, a few macaroons of bitter almonds, a teaspoonful of orange flower water, a little salt, a pint of cream, a glass of milk, & the yolks of five very fresh Eggs. Mix the whole well; & clarify 2 ozs of butter, & with a hoop of clean paper put some into the pancake pan, put a very little of the mixture into the pan at a time; let it be well done on the one side only, & turn the first one on the bottom of a silver plate, & do the same alternately with the others; arrange them in an agreeable form, & when you are about finishing, glaze the last with fine sugar, & salamander it; put the plate on a dish & send it up very hot. If you have a very hot oven ready, you may put the pancakes in for a few minutes—after which glaze them a l'Alexandre & serve very hot.

111 *Pancakes*

Put into a pan four spoonfuls of very fine flour, a pinch of salt, a spoonful of fine sugar, The peel of a lemon chopped very fine, & two eggs; dilute the whole of this with a pint of cream, melt a small bit of butter in a stew pan, throw it into the preparation, & then have a pancake pan very clean, put a very small bit of butter into it, let it get hot, put a spoonful of the mixture into the pan, turn round the pan, that the pancake may be done equally, then give a sudden jerk to turn the pancake on the other side; let it be well done on both sides; lastly, roll & glaze them with fine sugar. They must be made quickly, & there must be many to make a dish. Under this head you find many varieties, all of which however, resolve themselves to this: In some you put apricot marmalade, or currant jelly &c They are all similar.

112 *The Manner of Melting Isinglass*

To melt a quarter of a pound of Isinglass. take a little more than a pint of water, into which throw the 12th part of the white of an Egg; beat the water well till it becomes white, thrown the Isinglass into that water, & lay it on the stove over a very slow fire. If you keep it cover'd it will melt more easily. Take care it does not burn, for then it can never be made clear, & besides would have an unpleasant taste.

For a larger quantity put more water, but not more white of Egg. some people put in the peel of a lemon which is wrong, you may squeeze the juice of a lemon if you wish the Isinglass to be clear, but for cream it is useless. Always put Isinglass cautiously; in order to make cream or jellies in perfection try a little in a mould. If the jelly should not be firm enough, add a little more Isinglass. It is impossible to determine the exact quantity that is required for creams or jellies, as the dishes & moulds are never of the same dimensions. the best method is by tasting.

---

113 *Italian Cream*

Boil a pint of cream with half a pint of milk, when it boils, throw in the peel of an orange & of a lemon, to infuse with half a quarter of a pound of sugar and a small pinch of salt. When the cream is impregnated with the flavour of the fruit mix & beat it with the yolks of 8 Eggs, & put it on the fire to acquire an equal thickness. As soon as it is thick enough, & the Eggs done, put a little melted Isinglass in it, strain it well through a Tammy, & put some of it into a small mould, to try if it is thick enough to be turned over. If not, add a little more Isinglass & put the preparation into a mould on Ice. When quite frozen & you wish to send it up, dip a towel into hot water, & rub it all round the mould, to detach the cream, and turn it upside down on a dish. By this means the cream is brighter, & the dish is not soiled. If you whip the cream before you put it into the mould, it makes it more delicate & mellow; but you do not put the Isinglass into the cream before the cream is nearly done. In concluding the article on creams, it is necessary to observe that by variations of flavour with the same preparation a number of changes may be made with the same recipe.

114 *Pine Apple Cream*

Infuse the rind of a pine apple in boiling cream, & proceed as usual for other fruit. you must only use the rind, for the pulp being acid, the cream would curdle.

---

115 *Jellies of Fruit*

It is to be observed that all Jellies made of red fruit must be worked cold, & be put on Ice very promptly If you use a tin mould it would alter the colour & spoil the taste, but if you use earthen moulds, the jellies will always both look & taste as they ought. It is also advisable to clarify Isinglass while it is melting, there is less waste, & the jellies have a brighter appearance.

---

116 *No. 1. Strawberry Jelly*

Put some strawberries into an earthen pan, squeeze them well with a new wooden spoon; mix some pounded sugar with the fruit & let them infuse for an hour, that the sugar may draw out all the juice; next pour in a little water. If the strawberries are very ripe, squeeze the juice of 2 lemons to restore the acid taste of the straw-berries, for such preparations as are too sweet are insipid. Put all this into a bag that is nearly new, that the juice may be strained clear & limpid, mix some melted Isinglass with the juice, but mind that the whole must be very cold. Now put half a spoonful of the Jelly into a mould over ice to ascertain of what substance it is. If thick enough, put the whole into the large mould in Ice, & cover it also with Ice, but no salt, for it would spoil the bright color of the Jelly. Some people clarify the sugar, & when it is quite limpid & very hot, they throw their strawberries into it. This method is good enough, but then the Jelly does not keep the taste of the fruit so well. you may try either way. When the strawberries have been infused in the sugar, & they have discharged their colour, strain them through a bag, mix the Isinglass & lay them in Ice. Cover the mould with Ice also.

117 [Raspberry Jelly]

Raspberries in the same way either hot or cold. the Isinglass must be thrown in very cold, but the best way of all is to put the fruit into the mortar with some sugar, & mix them together, add a little water, put the whole into a jelly bag, & when the juice has been through, mix the cold Isinglass with it. press the fruit to extract the juice but do not break the seeds of the fruit as they would destroy the cleanliness of the Jelly.

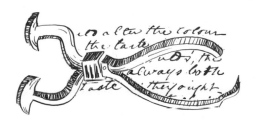

118 Orange Jelly

18 oranges are requisite to make a good jelly. peel lightly 6 oranges, & throw the peel into a little water, which lay on a corner of a stove, without allowing it to boil, lest it should taste too bitter. cut the oranges in two: have a silk sieve & a lemon squeezer, both of which dip into cold water, or otherwise they would absorb the juice of two oranges at least. Squeeze the oranges into the sieve over an earthen pan. This being done, pour the infusion of the peel through the sieve; next take a pound of sugar or so, in proportion to the acidity of the oranges, break it in a confectionary pan, pour a drop of the white of an Egg into about a pint of water, whip it 'till it gets white, pour it over the sugar & set it on the fire. When the sugar becomes frothy or scummy, throw a little more water in. Skim the sugar, let it reduce till it begins to bubble: & then pour in the juice of the oranges. The heat of the sugar will clarify the jelly. Do not let it boil, but as soon as you perceive a yellow scum, skim it & pour the jelly into a bag. next mix some melted Isinglass, either hot or cold. This jelly must not be made too firm, & especially avoid introducing any colour into it as it is almost always yellow. If the oranges are too ripe, mix a little lemon juice to make them acid. Lemon jelly the same way except a greater quantity of sugar.

119 *Jelly & Miroton of Peaches à la Mode*

Cut a dozen of peaches into halves, peel them gently, & boil them in a thin syrup but do not boil them too long   If they are very fine you may use them almost raw, but if common fruit the syrup will improve the look of them. break the stones, peel the kernels & throw them into the hot syrup with the fruit. When the peaches have infused about an hour, you may use them for making jelly en miroton, which is done as follows: drain the peaches in a new sieve, take the syrup, & squeeze six lemons into it; put this through a jelly bag; when very clear, put some clarified Isinglass into it, & put some into a plain mould in Ice. When it is firm, dress the peaches over the Jelly, & put the kernels between, then stick all this together with some jelly, when stiff, put some more jelly gently, let it freeze, & then fill the mould; put a great quantity of Ice around the mould, & some salt, as this Jelly is very liable to break, but it is one of the most delicate that can possibly be made. When you can not procure peaches fine enough to appear in the jelly you may make it as directed but by filtering thro' paper or a jelly bag, & mixing afterwards with the Isinglass you will obtain one of the best jellies possible.

---

120 *[Calves Feet Jelly]*

In making calves feet Jelly it is apt to break   When you turn your mould upside down in a dish. to prevent this throw in a pinch of Isinglass when you are going to clarify the jelly. It gives a greater substance.

121 *Fromage D'Apricots*

It will be necessary to premise that there is but little difference in the manner of making Fromages. They only vary in the taste. If in the summer season, take according to the size of them, 8 or 12 ripe apricots. take away the peel & stones. throw the Apricots into a mortar, & pound them with a little sugar. When well pounded rub them through a Tammy, & press upon the fruit with a new wooden spoon. Mix a little melted Isinglass with this puree. beat a pint of thick cream well, & mix it with the Apricots also. Taste whether the cream is sweetened enough. Continue to whip it over ice, till you perceive that the Isinglass is well melted & blended with the mixture. then put the fromage into a mould, round which you heap a large quantity of Ice with salt. If you do not particularly attend to the stirring of it over Ice, the apricots will fall to the bottom of the mould, so that when you turn the Ice cream upside down into the dish, it will appear of two colors, & the yellow part will be tough. In winter take a pot of Apricot marmalade rub it into a puree through a hair sieve   mix a little pounded sugar with it, & a little melted Isinglass. Then as above take a pint of thick cream, or more, according to the size of the mould, whip it well, mix it gently over Ice with the fruit, & when they are well mixed, put them into the mould, & surround it with Ice.

---

122 *Fromage of Strawberries*

Take a pottle of Strawberries   make a pureé of them, put a sufficient quantity of sugar to sweeten it well, & add a little clarified Isinglass. next mix the whole with a pint of whipped cream & proceed as directed above. of Raspberries the same.

---

123 *Fromage of Pine Apples*

If you have any pine apples left, you should mince them & make an infusion in a very little syrup, till they begin to be tender, then take them out of the sugar & pound them very fine in the mortar, add the juice of one lemon, & rub them through a tammy, with a little of the syrup, then whip your cream as before directed. Add the Isinglass to it, mix all together & put it in the mould as you do other cheeses.

124 *Peach Cheese*

Proceed as in the preceding. Infuse the Peaches in a little syrup, when they become tender, drain them; put the kernels in the mortar, & pound very fine; then put the peaches in the sieve rub them through with the almonds of the peaches, & mix that with the cream as above.

---

125 *Fromage of Orange Flowers*

In this case you must make an infusion, boil half a pint of cream, into which throw a handful of orange flowers, & let the cream cool. When it is cold, & has acquired the taste of the flowers, strain it through a sieve, & mix it with another pint of thick cream; keep whipping it over ice till the mixture is made thick. next take some melted Isinglass, & mix it well with some pounded sugar; put the whole with the cream; keep stirring it over the Ice till it acquires a good substance. Then fill the mould and surround it with Ice. N.B. fromages require but very little Isinglass, they must be very delicate & above all extremely cold.

---

126 *Fromage of Vanilla*

Here again you must make a decoction. Boil half a pint of cream; & infuse 2 sticks of Vanilla, cut into halves; add a little salt & sugar. for the rest proceed as before No. 6. Vanilla will serve twice if you pound the sticks the second time.

---

127 *Coffee Cream*

A pint of cream & a pint of milk, boil them together When boiled throw in a lump of sugar & a little salt. next roast the coffee in a coffee roaster, when well & equally roasted throw it burning hot into the cream, cover the stew pan, & let it infuse till it gets quite cold. If you wish to pour the cream into cups or any other small vessels, you must measure the quantity of cream but for a mould it is unnecessary, put the yolk of an egg to every cup rub the cream twice through a Tammy, in order that the egg may be well mixed with it, next put the cups into a pan containing water enough to reach to half the height of them; cover them, & put a little fire over the lid of the pan to prevent any steam dropping into the cream. as soon as it is done, let it cool & take care to secure the cups from dust &c. When you make the cream in a large mould, put more eggs.

128 *Lemon Cream*

The same for Lemon cream except instead of coffee, the peel of a lemon. if for moulds of large size use 16 Eggs for 2 pints cream or milk. the same in coffee cream.

---

129 *Orange Flower Cream*

Boil a pint of milk & a pint of cream, throw in a little salt, & more sugar. When the cream boils infuse a large pinch of orange flowers & when the cream has got the orange flavour give it a boil, put 10 yolks of very fresh Eggs & proceed as usual upon the fire, 'till the cream becomes thick; then put in the Isinglass &c. if your mould is small—8 Eggs are sufficient.

---

130 *Fromage au Café*

See creams for the mode of infusing the coffee. only use one half of the cream for the infusion, which when cold mix with the other half beat the whole on Ice, add Isinglass, then fill the mould.

131 *Marbled Jellies*

If you have a little orange Jelly left, & have any cream à la Venitienne, keep this latter in a very cool place, cut it into unequal pieces, the same as the orange jelly, put the whole into a mould & shake them together a little. When the pieces are well mixed, pour a little melted orange jelly into the mould. it must be quite cold to be nice.

132 *Clements Rolls. Excellent*

A quart of flour, one Egg, a tablespoonful or teaspoonful of butter. Mix it with a little milk, very stiff. beat it well. with an axe or very heavy weight, break off a small lump   roll it in your hand round, & bake it quick   do not roll out the dough.

---

133 *Remedy for the Bites of Snakes & Other Venemous Reptiles*

Take 2 parts of Sal Ammoniac   dissolve in 4 parts of warm water; then add one part of quick lime. put them together. shake them about 20 minutes; let the mixture settle & pour off the clear liquid. 2 teaspoonfuls to be taken in a cup of water, as soon after the accident as possible, & the dose repeated every three or four hours until the patient is out of danger.

---

134 *Cure for Consumption*

An English chemist of high fame, Mr John Murray of Hull. F.S.A. &c &c has at length discover'd what he firmly believes to be a cure for tubercular phthisis. for fargone consumption. His work on this subject, which is dedicated to the Duke of Wellington, contains the result of 12 years inquiry, during which period his thoughts have been exclusively bent to this noble & philanthropic object. In the progress of his investigations, he came to the very rational conclusion, & one which has impressed many other minds, that if any remedy should ever be found out for structural disease of the lungs, it must be some one which may be brought, through the medium of respiration, into immediate contact with the diseased surface, &, when there, have the power of subduing the morbid action, without diminishing the general tone of the system. At length Mr Murray believes that he has discover'd such a remedy in the *vapour of nitric acid*; & this fact is the more worthy of attention, since it comes from a source where empiricism cannot be suspected. Mr Murray is well known in the scientific world as author of some valuable works on chemistry & has, we believe, been himself a sufferer from the scourge he has striven so sedulously to avert.

Boston Medical and Surgical Journal.

135 *French Cake*

5 common sized tumblers of sifted flour, 3 tumblers of powder'd white sugar, half a tumbler of butter, one tumbler rich milk or
cream, a teaspoonful of pearl ash dissolved in as much luke warm
water as will cover it. mix all well together in a pan. Beat 3 eggs
together 'till very light, then add them to the mixture throw in a
tea spoonful of powder'd cinnamon or nutmeg, beat the whole very
hard about 10 minutes. Butter a deep pan put in the mixture &
bake it in a moderate oven.

---

136 *For Snake Bite*

2 table spoonfuls of fresh Chloride of Lime in powder mix
it with half a pint of water, & with this wash keep the wound constantly bathed, & frequently renewed. The chlorine gas possesses
the power of decomposing this tremendous poison, & renders mild
& harmless that venom against whose resistless attack the artillery of
medical science has been so long directed in vain. It is necessary to
apply this wash as soon as possible after the bite.

---

137 *For Croup*

Equal parts of camphor, spirits of wine & hartshorn well
mixed together.

---

138 *For Bleeding at the Nose*

10 grs Sugar of Lead, 60 grs white Vitriol dissolved in half a
pint of water snuff it up into the nostrils out of the palm of the
hand. If that fails dip a soft rag in the mixture, roll it in fine charcoal
& stuff it up the nose.

Dr Henderson's Recipe.

139 *Peppers. Mrs Coxe*

put them in strong salt & water 'till they are yellow   then green them in Vinegar & water, half & half over the fire, great care is necessary to watch them & prevent the water getting more than blood heat—that it is which makes them grow soft. As soon as they are green, boil some very strong vinegar & pour it warm on them stuff some if you like after greening them.

140 *Recipe for Mrs Waite's Gingerbread*

1 lb of flour, 1 pint of molasses
1 lb of brown sugar, 1/2 lb of butter

half a cup of Ginger, 4 Eggs, teaspoonful of Sal aratus or Potash. season with spice to your taste. Bake in a large pan.

141 *Old Dolls Method of Washing Color'd Dresses*

Wash them in two lathers of milk warm water, rinse them in fair water milk warm   then have ready their starch enough to wet the whole dress. 3 table spoonfuls of starch to half a handful of salt, make it thick, & thin it afterwards. run the dress through it, & hang it out to dry—starching with salt prevents the colour from running.

142 *Clements Rolls. Best Recipe*

half a pint of milk
a quart of flour,
1 Egg
a teaspoonful of butter
a tablespoonful of yeast,

warm the milk & Egg enough to melt the butter, put half the flour in a pot, add the yeast   mix the milk, Egg & butter with the flour & yeast to the consistency of batter, put it by at night to rise. next morning put the other pint of flour on a board & mix all well together, put it by to lighten & bake them quick after making it into rolls.

143 *To Wash Flannels*

In washing flannels—make a lather of milk warm water wash them in this, & in two more lathers of milk warm water   then wring out the suds & hang out to dry. never rinse in cold or fair water, it makes the flannel shrink.

---

144 *Tomato Figs*

6 lbs of sugar, clean brown, to 16 lbs of Tomatoes, scald & skin them in the usual way   simmer them over the fire (their own juice is sufficient without the addition of water) until the sugar penetrates, & they are clarified. They are then taken out spread on dishes, flatten'd & dried in the sun. a small quantity of the syrup should be occasionally sprinkled over them while drying, when dry pack them in boxes, sifting powder'd sugar over them. The Syrup is boiled afterwards & bottled for use. They keep well from year to year & retain their flavour which is nearly that of the best fresh figs. the pear shaped or single tomato answers best.

---

145 *For Worms. Mrs G Wn.*

1 oz seeds of wormseed
half an oz Rhubarb
1 tablespoon small cloves of garlic,

   put the ingredients into a pint bottle   fill it with best wine or whiskey, let it stand a few days, shaking it well, then strain it. for a child of 5 years a small teaspoonful, less for younger children.

---

146 *Isinglass Jelly*

Cut 3 good sized Lemons in thin slices with the skin on, one pound of white sugar, 2 quarts of cold water, 2 ozs of Isinglass (first soak the Isinglass in cold water for half an hour), 1 stick of Cinnamon, a little mace & orange peel. add the whites of 4 Eggs & shells, a pint of wine   madeira   & stir them well with all the other ingredients, boil the whole a few minutes, & then pour it through a thick flannel Jelly bag. the bottom of the Bag 8 or 10 inches wide across the bottom. the liquor that runs through first should be pour'd back into the Bag until it runs clear.

147 *For Blanc Mange*

one oz of Isinglass for 2 quarts of milk or cream, peels of 2 Lemons, sugar & spice, cinnamon & mace, to your taste, make it boil, strain it   stir it when nearly cool to mix the cream that rises, while cooling wet the moulds with cold water to prevent sticking spoon in your Blanc Mange.

---

148 *To Make Lemon Cordial*

Take one dozen good sized Lemons, cut them up   put them in a gallon bottle and fill it up with old whiskey. let it stand two Months   it is best to shake it up frequently. pour it off from the fruit and fill the Bottle with soft water and let it remain four weeks, add that to the spirit, then take 4 pounds of sugar   disolve it in as much water as will enable you to clarify it. add the surip to the whole with the adition of one pint of lime juice.

---

149 *Dolcey's Mode of Doing up Muslin, Silk, Camb[ric]k, Stuff*

Muslin, Cambk, & common clothes (except flannel)—wash in two waters as hot as you can bear it with hard soap, strong suds then boil in blue water until white—if very yellow they must be rubbed with hard soap when put into the Kettle. the water must be just warm in the kettle when the clothes are put in. Then well boiled. When white enough take them out, wring & dry them—for *thin* muslin use very thick starch, for thick muslin & cambk very thin—squeeze out the starch, wring them in old linen or diaper, then dry them again   the cambk must be sprinkled before it is ironed. the muslin must only be clapped until perfectly clear, then placed smooth with the hands & ironed when dry. muslin should always be boiled in a brown linen bag not too thick—brown rolls is the best. dresses never boiled with anything but muslin articles. silk, stuff, colord clothes & flannel must be washed twice in milk warm suds then wrung out clear, roll'd smooth. silk & stuff iron'd on the wrong side before they are dry—this gives a gloss. color'd clothes sprinkled & iron'd as cambks. flannel smooth'd with the hands after shaking them a little then hung out to dry. silk hose done up as other silks. white are ting'd with pink by drop cake made like blue water. Black crape is washed in clear water then stiffen'd with gum arabic, clapped & very lightly ironed. color'd winter vests in milk warm suds, twice, iron'd when damp, on the wrong side.

150 *To Destroy the Bee Worm or Bee Miller*

Have the bottom edges of the Hives, so thin as to afford them no shelter. during the warm weather raise the Hive by placing small sticks around under the Hive so as to raise it half an inch from the bench on which the Hive is placed. these take out during the cold months.
Milcy Hamilton's letter to J S Skinner Esq [?] Editor of the A[merican].
Farmer.

151 *Chinese Mode of Mending China*

Boil a piece of white flint glass in river water for five or six minutes, beat it to a fine powder, & grind it well in the white of an egg, & it joins the China without rivetting, so that no art can break it again in the same place. Observe the composition must be ground extremely fine on a painters slab.

152 *Hive Syrup*

Of the Hive Syrup children may take from ten or twenty drops, to one or more teaspoonfuls three times a day, regulating the size of dose so that a little vomiting may be produced at first, and afterward diminish it so as to avoid puking.
Resp[ectfull]y E. Stabler

153 *Chloride of Lime in Mad Dog Bites*

The wound is to be washed as soon as possible with a solution of Chloride of Lime, & the liquid should be injected into it with a syringe. cover the wound with a piece of Lint impregnated with the solution. repeat the treatment twice a day till the wound cicatrizes. but if it should not heal in five days it is then to be treated in the ordinary manner. If the wound has healed before employing the chloride it is to be cauterized with the butter of antimony & when the eschar separates the lotion is to be used. During the first five days the solution of the chloride must be taken internally in doses of half a teaspoonful or more as the stomach will bear it 3 times a day in an ounce of sweeten'd water. This remedy is said (in an article in the "Courier des Etats Unis") to be useful in the bite of venemous snakes, used as a lotion with the syringe.

To prepare the Chloride when in powder. Our friend E. Lewis is respectfully informed that the proper method of preparing the solution of chloride of lime is the following—th. chloride in a mortar with succession small portions of Water until it is all dissolved. add all the waters together   let the liquid stand until it is clear, then decant it into bottles which must be kept closely stopped, for on exposure to air the active principle leaves it. We know very little of the internal use of this remedy yet but would advise if a case occur urgently demanding its exhibition that it should be given in doses of a small teaspoonful two or three times a day, or more or less, acc'g to the effect it produces.

The effects of Chloride of Soda & Chloride of Lime are similar. Lime is cheapest. There is a remedy for snake bites which is strongly recommended should this fail of success. that is the strongest water of Ammonia (Aqua Ammonia Fortius). a very intelligent Physician of Mississippi professes to have used this with almost invariable success during a long practice, & we have known for many years that analagous treatment cures the bite of the venemous spider. The Physician spoken of directs that the part wounded by a rattle snake, mocassin, viper &c should be first well washed with warm water, then a perdget of Lint wetted with the volatile liquid should be applied, & that the patient should take a teaspoonful of it in a wine glassful of cold water   The whole operation, except the washing, should be repeated every half hour, or hour until relief shall be obtained.

154 *For the Scurvy*

Take of Tincture of Alleppo Salts and Tincture of Myrrh—equal parts. after every meal first wash the teeth with a brush & then wet the gums with the above liquid either pure or diluted with water.

---

155 *[For Mad Dog Bites]*

For using with a Syringe in bites of mad dogs—1 lb Chloride of Lime, dissolved in 10 pints of water bottled or put into a jug close stopped.

156 *[For Room Odours]*

To a pound of Chloride of Lime in powder add forty pints of water   Mix by degrees, sprinkle the walls & floors of apartments where sickness has prevailed or in cellars &c where any bad odour is found.

---

157 *[Chloride of Soda]*

In relieving persons affected by bad air from offensive servers &c a napkin moisten'd with Chloride of Soda placed under the nostrils & repeated restored several from apparent death, it arrests mortification, heals wounds, modifys cancerous & other tropical complaints.

158 *Old Letty's Peach Chips*

Pare & slice moderately thin your peaches   fill your skillet with them, sprinkle over half a pound of sugar, just boil them stirring well until scalded through—then take them out with your skimmer & fill your skillet with more peaches   scald those thro' well & fill again   sprinkle in half a pint of sugar, & as often as your syrup is *sour* add half a pint of sugar until all your peaches are scalded. as they are taken out of the skillet spread them on pewter dishes, & put them into the Sun; as you turn them over sprinkle them with sugar every day until perfectly dry. then pack them in your pot, with sugar sprinkled between the layers—tie up for use. a peck of peaches will scald one pound of sugar—not soft peaches or too ripe. If liquor is left, you can add more sugar & fresh peaches.

---

159 *[For Ring Worms]*

a salve made of ginger & rosin soap, rubbed on ring worms, will kill them.

---

160 *Recipe for Making Red Beads*

Take the crumb of stale rye bread without any mixture of flour. Moisten it with spirits of hartshorn, and colour with vermillion.

---

161 *For the Tooth Ache*

Burnt Alum, black pepper & ginger equal parts, ground together, add spirits of camphor. dip a piece of lint in the mixture & fill the hollow tooth by means of a blunt needle. It has cured more than a thousand times.

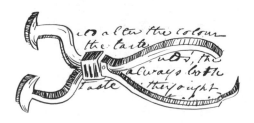

162 *[For the Tooth Ache]*

forceps plain, right angled & straight with cutting edges, like the surgical bone forceps, made accurately to fit the necks of the teeth & only the necks. however decayed the tooth may be will cut them off safely & without pain, leaving the root sound in the gum to chew upon or screw a new tooth to—& is much less injurious to the sound teeth remaining than extraction.

163 *Flaxseed Syrup*

To half a pint of flaxseed add a quart of water, boil it down to a pint, strain it, & add sugar candy & liquorice Stew them together & when done, squeeze in a little Lemon juice, & about a table spoonful of french Brandy—if you like to add brandy. it is most excellent for colds & coughs.

164 *Dr Becker of Berlin on Cholera*

The remedies I chiefly employ'd were acid baths, camphor, external heat, & other stimuli, leeches & bleeding. Indian Cholera. It is proved *contagious* beyond all doubt—conveyed by clothing, goods, & any thing used by or within the Influence of persons ill or dead of the disease—rigid quarantine regulations will arrest its progress. articles once infected must be purified by heat, immersion, & fumigation. fumigation alone will not destroy the contagation.

1832.

contagion may remain many days even weeks inert, but active means alone will remove it. *rigid quarantine* is the best security.

165 *Cholera. Prince Lievin's Remedy*

The moment the least symptom of approach of the Cholera, from 20 to 30 drops of Laudanum the same quantity of Ether to be taken in camphor Julip, or peppermint water; rhubarb or tincture of Rhubarb to be taken if necessary; but on no account Salts or magnesia; then send for medical advice No case has proved fatal with these precautions. a person in the Liverpool Mercury by name Taylor calls this Melanaema or black blood disease & prescribes the inhalation of Oxygen gas.

166 *Compound Chlorine Tooth Wash*

Turn a teaspoonful into a tumbler, common size, & add water till it is one third full. Rinse the mouth & apply it to the teeth with your brush. Shake the Bottle well before using & be careful to keep it well corked. It is most excellent for sore mouths, swelled & spongy gums, bad breath, & disagreeable effects from salivation. It is prepared by Lowe & Reed, Boston & put up in mould bottles. each bottle is stamped "Lowe & Reeds Compd Chlorine tooth wash" & the seal is stamped   attached to each is the signature of "Lowe & Reed" in the hand writing of the firm.

---

167 *Muffin Bread*

A pint of flour, half a pint of bolted meal, 2 table spoonfuls of yeast, a small table spoon of fresh butter. All the white & half the yolk of an Egg, make it up with milk at night, the thickness of wheat loaf bread   in the morning bake it in a tin pan.

---

168 *Muffins*

Take a quart of risen dough in the morning, add to it an Egg well beaten, the dough must be thinner than that for loaves & rolls, if the Egg does not thin it enough add 2 table spoonfuls of milk warm water. cut it out with a spoon—a table spoonful for each muffin, butter the gridle & put them onto bake, turn them with a knife   the gridle must be hot enough to bake bread on.

---

169 *Batter Cakes*

3 pints of sifted meal; add one Egg well beaten to a quart of milk. the milk put by degrees to the Egg   then stir all in by degrees to the meal. bake like the muffins.

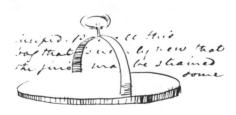

170 *Valuable Recipes in the Honfleur Painting*

Horn paper for formula's or Theorems is thus made. Letter paper or good foolscap is cover'd with a coat of boiled Linseed oil & spirits of turpentine, (say in about equal proportions) for the purpose of making it transparent. When dry successive coats of the best copal varnish are laid on until the coat is thick enough. Both sides of the paper should be coated.

The mixing fluid for grinding the paints (in powder/on ground glass palettes), is made by dissolving Gum Tragacanth in water to the proper consistency which is like thin gum arabic water, not *very* thin.

---

171 *For Making Lead Cups*

Grind on a a slab any quantity of mexican lead with a convenient proportion of weak mucilage Gum Arabic, then coat the cups with it in the inside & suffer them to dry. This is for Honfleur's mezzotinto. put on with a scrub brush with very little water for the first coat, the darker shades with a little more water, but less than for the color'd paintings & the fine strokes done with lead pencils stamped "prepared No's 2 & 3". You vein color'd paintings with a hair brush & Gum water with the paints.

---

172 *Directions for Painting on Wood. Miss Selden of Norfolk*

There is but little difference between painting on wood & paper. the same paints are used & the same brushes, but instead of water the paints are rubbed up with a thin size of Isinglass. with carmine & other transparent colors you use a small quantity of white lead (or flake white). The Isinglass size is used altogether instead of water. The articles may be varnished when perfectly dry.

From Mrs Talcott.

---

173 *New Orleans Remedy for Sore Throat*

boil Potatoes soft with peels on mash them quick put them in a piece of linen hot bind them to the throat, when cold renew the hot potatoes.

174 *To Make Currant Wine*

Wash your currants & strain off the juice through a flannel bag, to every gal of the juice add 3 gals of soft water, & to every gal of mixture add 3 lbs N Orleans sugar & half a pint of french Brandy. fill your cask & put it in a cool cellar to ferment. When the fermentation is going on, every morning fill up the cask with cold water that the froth & impurities may work out of the bung hole, which may be lightly cover'd with a thin rag to prevent flies from getting in. as soon as the fermentation is over bung the cask up tight, & let it remain so for one year, when it may be bottled up or drawn on tap. The only material difference between this & other recipes, is, the addition of the Brandy before the fermentation takes place—upon which the goodness of the wine in a great measure depends. The fermentation proceeds slowly, without violence, as soon as it is ended, which is in 20 days. The bung is stopped, a peg put loose in the gimblet hole for a week or two that some of the fixed air might escape, & then driven in tight.

---

175 *More Grape Wine*

To every bushel of fox grapes add 22 quarts of water, mash the fruit   let it stand 24 hours, strain it through linen & to every gallon of juice add 2 lbs of brown sugar, fill the cask 3 fourths full, let it stand open 14 days then close the bung.

---

176 *Almond Cream*

one quart of cream sweeten'd with half a pint of white sugar, boiled up with vanilla 2 pods, have ready half a pint of blanched almonds ground with a quarter of a pint of white powderd sugar by degrees to prevent oiling, 8 yolks of Eggs beaten very lightly stirred into the cream, you add a little cream to the Eggs, & a little to the almonds & mix them up well   stir first the Eggs & then the Al- monds into the cream (just before the mixture boils) you pour it off.

Glossary

alkanet: root of wild bugloss, *Alkanna tinctoria*; provided a bright red coloring agent used in dyes, medicine, furniture polish, and cosmetics.

almond of peaches: almond-shaped soft interior portion of the peach kernel; often used interchangeably with almonds.

alum: double sulfate of ammonium; commonly used in medicine as an astringent and emetic and in dyeing as a mordant, combining with organic dyes to form an insoluble color compound.

alum basket: cane or wire frame encrusted with crystallized alum for a rock candy effect; a nineteenth-century home decorating fancy.

aqua fortis: nitric acid; called aqua fortis (literally, strong water) because it was one of the most corrosive substances known to early science, eating away almost any substance with which it came into contact, including all the metals except gold.

balsam peru: aromatic and soothing gum resin exuded by a Latin American tree, *Myroxylon balsamum*; used in medicinal ointments and skin lotions.

bee miller: moth with dusty-looking wings; a pest to honey raisers because it laid its eggs in hives where its larvae fed on the honey comb and young bees.

blade mace: fleshy crimson-colored aril, or extra covering, on the seed of the nutmeg, *Myristica fragrans*; peeled off, dried, and sold separately as a blade of mace.

blood heat: lukewarm.

blue water: rinse water tinted with indigo.

bolted meal: sifted meal.

butter of antimony: metallic chloride used by nineteenth-century physicians to raise a blister on the skin.

cambric: fine, thin linen or linen-like cotton cloth commonly used for summer dresses and men's shirts.

camphor: whitish, crystalline substance derived from the camphor tree; used in medicine as an irritant and stimulant.

carmine: crimson pigment obtained from cochineal.

chloride of lime: white powder obtained by treating slaked lime with chlorine; used for disinfecting, bleaching, and cleaning.

chloride of soda: common salt; in the uses suggested in the manuscript, perhaps a misnomer for ammonium chloride.

cholera: any of a number of intestinal diseases. Cholera morbus is a noninfectious, seldom fatal disease, characterized by cramps and diarrhea; it is often caused by contaminated food. Asiatic cholera is an infectious, often fatal, disease caused by a microorganism. It is characterized by severe vomiting and diarrhea, cramps and collapse; it is spread by lack of personal hygiene and contaminated water supplies.

citron: oldest of the citrus fruits, resembling a lemon but with a very thick warty greenish-yellow peel and sour small pulp. The peel is treated with brine to remove the bitter oil and bring out the flavor; then it is candied in sugar and used in baking.

cochineal: dried bodies of the insect, *Coccus cacti*, which lives on the Mexican prickly pear; used in dyeing to obtain brilliant scarlet and crimson hues.

consumption: tuberculosis.

copal varnish: varnish made from hard lustrous resin of tropical trees.

copperas: ferrous sulfate, a green, crystalline compound; used in dyeing to produce dark shades.

cordial: term applied to a medicine, food, or beverage that was considered either literally or figuratively invigorating or comforting to the heart.

cressi (Crécy): vegetable purée which includes carrots or soup made from such a purée; named for Crécy in the Seine-et-Marne, long known for the excellent quality of its carrots.

croup: any affection of the larynx or trachea characterized by a hoarse cough and difficult breathing; in the nineteenth century often a misnomer for diphtheria.

cruller: fried cake, similar to a doughnut.

currants: tiny dried seedless grapes, smaller and darker than raisins, used chiefly in baking; the name was a corruption of Corinth, the Greek city from where they originated.

decoction: extraction and concentration of the essence of a substance, for example, lemon or coffee, by boiling.

drachm: see dram.

Dragon's blood: resin extracted from the berries of the Dragon's Blood Palm, *Daemomoropa draco*, and formed into balls or sticks for sale; used as a dark red coloring agent in varnishes, stains and medicines.

dram: $1/8$ oz. in apothecaries or troy weight. This standard of weight evolved for the regulated weighing of valuable items, such as gold, jewels, and drugs, in the great medieval trading center of Troyes, France. Bulky and cheap items, such as potatoes and coal, were measured by avoirdupois weight, in which a dram is $1/16$ oz.

eschar: dry scab that forms as the result of a burn or an injury from a corrosive substance.

ether: volatile liquid derived from the action of sulfuric acid on ethyl alcohol; used as a solvent in some medicines.

flake white: pigment made from pure white lead.

flaxseed: seed of any of several species of *Linaria*, a wild hardy annual; used to make linseed oil and prescribed in medicine as an astringent.

float of indigo: see indigo.

foolscap: writing paper, usually folded, varying in size from $12'' \times 15''$ to $12\frac{1}{2}'' \times 16''$.

fox grape: North American wild grapes; the species native to the south is *Vitis rotundifolia*.

fromage: cheese; by extension, a molded cream-based dessert.

fustic: wood of a tropical American tree, *Chlorophora tinctoria*, producing a bright orange-yellow dye. Large logs were imported and split into chips which were used when yellow, green, olive, or drab hues were desired.

gill: unit of liquid measure, equal to $1/4$ pint.

gum arabic: gum naturally exuded by *Acacia senegal* and other acacia trees. It was collected, powdered, and later mixed with water to make a thick, mucilaginous solution used in making inks, mucilage, paints, dyes and starch. In medicine it served as a demulcent, soothing and protecting irritated mucous membranes.

gum tragacanth: gum obtained from a Persian shrub, *Astalagus*; used in paints and medicines.

hair sieve: sieve made of split wood or metal with an inset net of horsehair; the close weaving of the horsehair made this a very fine sieve.

hartshorn: antler of the male deer; shaved to obtain ammonia, used in smelling salts, and a type of gelatin, used to make jelly for invalids.

Honfleur painting: a style of painting taught by Mme. Honfleur in Richmond, Va., during the 1830s.

hops: dried ripe cones of the female flowers of the hop plant; used in making yeast and in brewing.

horn paper: paper which was made transparent by a treatment of resin and alcohol.

Indian meal: corn meal.

indigo: blue-purple dye derived from the tropical plant, *Indigofera tinctoria*; one of the finest and longest lasting of the natural dyes. The best grade of indigo, which was imported from Latin America, was called a float or floaton of indigo because it was a fine, soft texture which floated to the surface of water; inferior or adulterated indigo sank to the bottom.

infusion: liquid extract that results from steeping or soaking a substance, for example, tea.

isinglass: form of gelatin prepared from the internal membranes of sturgeon bladders.

jumbles (jumbals): thin, flat banquet or tea cakes. Early versions of jumbals were worked in interlaced rings and knots similar to a double-finger ring popular in the sixteenth century, known as *gimbel* or *gemmel* from the Latin, *geminus*, twin.

lard: white solid or semisolid rendered fat of a hog.

laudanum: solution of opium in alcohol widely used in the nineteenth century to relieve pain.

linseed oil: drying oil used in making paints and inks.

lint: soft, fleecy material made by carding linen; used as a poultice or dressing for wounds.

loaf sugar: large, solid cone of refined sugar usually weighing nine to ten pounds.

logwood: dark heartwood of a tropical tree, *Haematoxylon campechianum*, commonly used by dyers because of its low cost and the great variety of black, dark blue, and dark brown shades obtained from it.

lye: solution resulting from pouring boiling water through wood ashes.

madder: root of the European plant, *Rubia tinctorum*, the source of a strong orange-red dye which resisted fading.

mezzotinto: half-tint or chiaroscuro; a style of painting in which extreme dark and light shades were contrasted; today, commonly refers to an engraving technique.

miroton: dish most commonly made from small pieces of meat; also a dish made of pieces of cut fruit.

Naples macaroni: common straight macaroni; so named because Naples was the center of the pasta industry.

oil mango: cantaloupe or other small muskmelon pickled so as to resemble the popular and expensive imported pickled mango.

oil of almonds: oil extracted from the poisonous bitter almond, *Amygdalus prunus* var. *amara*; used in small quantities for flavoring food and in skin emollients.

oil of vitriol: sulfuric acid.

orange flower water: liquid distilled from orange blossoms.

pearl ash: potassium carbonate, used in baking as a leavening agent. It was obtained by purifying potash through heating and recrystallization; its white color gave rise to the name ashes of pearls or pearl ash.

pledget: compress or small flat mass, usually of gauze or absorbent cotton, placed over a wound.

potash: potassium carbonate, used in baking as a leavening agent. The powdery ash was obtained by boiling wood ash and water in large iron pots, until only a dry residue remained.

pottle: unit of liquid measure, equivalent to two quarts.

Queensware: durable, cream-colored glazed earthenware by Wedgewood which was very popular on the world market during the eighteenth and nineteenth centuries; name acquired when Josiah Wedgewood secured the patronage of Queen Charlotte in 1765.

quicklime: white caustic lumpy powder obtained by rapidly heating limestone in a furnace.

race ginger: hand of ginger, one portion of the large ginger rhizome.

rasp: grate.

redwood (Brazil wood): dyewood from the tropical tree, *Caesalpinia echinata*; used to obtain reddish shades ranging from pink to violet.

rhubarb: dried root of common garden rhubarb, *Rheum rhaponticum*; an effective natural laxative.

rose pink: coloring agent producing hues from light purplish pink to a strong pink.

rose water: liquid distilled from rose petals, carrying the scent and flavor of roses; used for thousands of years in cookery and cosmetics.

rosin soap: hard soap to which the brittle resin of the pine tree was added.

salamander: long-handled iron tool with a flat broad end that was heated red hot and then held over food to brown the top.

sal ammoniac: ammonium chloride, a white granular powder used medically and industrially.

sal aratus (saleratus): sodium bicarbonate; used as a leavening agent in baking.

saltpeter: potassium nitrate, a transparent white crystalline compound used in curing meat. It has a more penetrating and drying effect on meat than salt alone and gives the meat a red color.

sassafras: native North American tree, *Sassafras albidum*; the aromatic bark of its root was used in making tea and flavoring medicine because of its pleasant scent and its supposed curative qualities.

scurvy: deficiency disease caused by lack of vitamin C in the diet; characterized by general bodily debility, tender gums and loose teeth, foul breath, and subcutaneous bleeding.

soft water: rain water or water to which a small amount of lye or potash has been added.

spermaceti: fatty substance found in the head of a sperm whale, used in cosmetics and skin ointments; formerly it was believed that the substance was the sperm of the whale.

spirits of turpentine: colorless oil distilled from turpentine; used in paints.

spirits of wine: purified ethyl alcohol.

sponge: the initial dough preparation for cakes and breads which is subsequently allowed to rise.

stuff: woven woolen material.

suet: hard, fatty tissues around the kidneys and loins of cattle and sheep.

sugar of lead: lead acetate, a poisonous white crystalline compound used in dyes and varnishes.

sumach (sumac): native American shrub, *Rhus glabra*, cultivated in Virginia for its dye. All portions of the plant could be processed to obtain sandy and pale orange hues and in combination with other dyes for dark shades.

sweet herbs: *fines herbes*, a combination of two or more finely chopped fresh herbs. The combination varied, but the most common herbs used were parsley, thyme, basil, chives, marjoram, bay leaf, and winter savory.

sweet oil: superior grade of olive oil imported from the Mediterranean countries; often called Florence oil.

tammy: flannel cloth stretched across a base through which stocks, soups, and purées were strained. Various thicknesses of cloth could be attached depending on the desired result.

theorem paper: black paper used in tracing designs for painting on velvet.

tincture of Alleppo salts: perhaps a solution of powdered Aleppo nutgalls. The gall is a growth on oaks in Aleppo, Syria; it is usually used in tanning, but because of its astringent qualities it might have been used in the treatment of loose teeth and sore gums caused by scurvy.

tincture of myrrh: solution of the aromatic and soothing gum resin obtained from *Commiphora myrrha*.

virgin wax: pure or refined wax.

water of ammonia: ammonium hydroxide, an ammonia solution used as a household cleaner.

white lead: basic lead carbonate, a white heavy powder used as a pigment.

white vitriol: zinc sulfate, a colorless crystalline compound used medically as an emetic and astringent; believed to be particularly effective in checking uncontrolled bleeding.

wormseed: small flowers and crushed fruit of the American wormseed, *Chenopodium ambrosioides*, a native perennial. Pharmacists extracted a drug from it which was made into lozenges or tablets which paralyzed and expelled round worms and thread worms from the digestive tract; it was also used with some success in cases of tapeworm and hookworm.

worsted: wool cloth with a hard smooth napless surface.

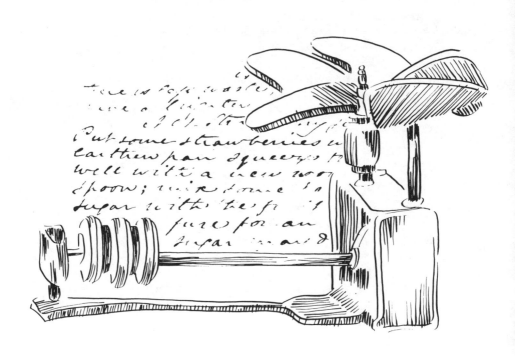

Bibliography

PRIMARY SOURCES

Mrs. Lewis's letters and those of her relatives, friends, and guests were indispensable in recapturing the rhythm of daily life at Woodlawn. Collectively, they reflected the subtle ebb and flow of domestic concerns. Incidental observations—what garden crop was in season, a run of fish in the river, special foods for a grand occasion, the purchase of more efficient and modern kitchen equipment, shared recipes and patterns, an illness and its treatment, the revolting table manners of an in-law—contributed piece by piece to the picture of life at Woodlawn.

The manuscripts division of the Historic New Orleans Collection holds the papers of the Butler family, including the housekeeping book itself, as well as numerous letters from members of the Lewis family to Frances or Edward Butler. During the early 1830s Mrs. Lewis wrote to her daughter especially often; these letters were very long and filled with the most minute domestic details.

The library of the Mount Vernon Ladies' Association of the Union also has a large number of Lewis family documents. Particularly valuable to this study was the extensive collection of Mrs. Lewis's letters to her friend, Elizabeth Bordley Gibson of Philadelphia. These frank and open letters spanned her lifetime, illuminating many aspects of her temperament and character development. Domestic affairs were often touched on as well, since Mrs. Lewis frequently asked her friend to buy household or personal items which were not available locally.

The study collection at Woodlawn Plantation includes Lewis family material and typescripts of letters from a number of visitors to Woodlawn. They described the house and grounds, the appearance and manners of family members, family entertainment, furniture, table settings, dinner parties, and servants.

SECONDARY SOURCES

Asimov, Isaac. *Words of Science and the History behind Them*. Boston, 1959.

Blanton, Wyndham B. *Medicine in Virginia in the Eighteenth Century*. Richmond, 1931.

———. *Medicine in Virginia in the Nineteenth Century*. Richmond, 1933.

Bronson, J. and R. *The Domestic Manufacturer's Assistant, and Family Directory in the Arts of Weaving and Dyeing.* Utica, 1817.

Bullock, Helen. *The Williamsburg Art of Cookery, or Accomplish'd Gentlewoman's Companion.* Williamsburg, Va., 1938.

Carson, Jane. *Colonial Virginia Cookery.* Williamsburg, Va., 1968.

———. *Colonial Virginians at Play.* Williamsburg, Va., 1965.

Cartwright, Frederick F. *Disease and History.* New York, 1972.

Confederate Receipt Book: A Compilation of Over One Hundred Receipts Adapted to the Times. Richmond, 1863; reprint ed., Athens, Ga., 1960.

Custis, George Washington Parke. *Recollections and Private Memoirs.* New York, 1860.

Earle, Alice M. *Child Life in Colonial Days.* New York, 1899.

———. *Colonial Dames and Good Wives.* New York, 1895.

———. *Home Life in Colonial Days.* New York, 1899.

Ellis, Asa, Jr. *The Country Dyer's Assistant.* Brookfield, Mass., 1798.

Flexner, James T. *Washington: The Indispensable Man.* Boston, 1969.

Freeman, Douglas Southall. *Washington.* 1 vol. abr. by Richard Harwell. New York, 1968.

Gill, Harold B., Jr. *The Apothecary in Colonial Virginia.* Williamsburg, Va., 1972.

Glasse, Hannah. *The Art of Cookery Made Plain and Easy.* London, 1796; reprint ed., Hamden, Conn., 1971.

Haagensen, C. D., and Wyndham E. B. Lloyd. *A Hundred Years of Medicine.* New York, 1943.

Harrison, S. G. *et al. The Oxford Book of Food Plants.* London, 1969.

Hartley, Dorothy. *Food in England.* London, 1954.

Hess, Karen. *Martha Washington's Booke of Cookery.* New York, 1981.

Hughes, Rupert. *George Washington; The Savior of the States, 1777-1781.* New York, 1930.

Hume, Audrey N. *Food.* Colonial Williamsburg Archaeological Series, No. 9. Williamsburg, Va., 1978.

Jackson, Donald. "George Washington's Beautiful Nelly." *American Heritage*, 28 (1977), 80-85.

Jackson, Donald, and Dorothy Twohig, eds. *The Diaries of George Washington.* 6 vols. Charlottesville, Va., 1976-1979.

Johnson, Gerald W. *Mount Vernon: The Story of a Shrine.* New York, 1953.

Kimball, Marie. *The Martha Washington Cook Book.* New York, 1940.

Latané, Polly Graham, and Joyce Graham [Taylor], comps. *The Old Washington Recipes.* N.p., 1931.

Lee, N. K. *The Cook's Own Book.* Boston, 1832.

Leslie, Eliza. *Miss Leslie's Lady's House-Book; A Manual of Domestic Economy.* 15th ed., enl. Philadelphia, 1852.

LeStrange, Richard. *A History of Herbal Plants.* New York, 1977.

Montague, Prosper. *Larousse Gastronomique.* Eds. Charlotte Turgeon and Nina Froud. New York, 1961.

Moore, Charles. *The Family Life of George Washington.* Boston, 1926.

Moore, Gay M. *Seaport in Virginia: George Washington's Alexandria.* Richmond, 1949.

Moore, Virginia. *Virginia Is a State of Mind.* New York, 1943.

Morgan, Edmund S. *Virginians at Home: Family Life in the Eighteenth Century.* Williamsburg, Va., 1952.

Mott, Frank L. *A History of American Magazines, 1741-1850.* New York, 1930.

Niemcewicz, Julian U. *Under Their Vine and Fig Tree.* Trans. and ed. Metchie J. E. Budka. Elizabeth, N.J., 1965.

Page, Thomas N. *Social Life in Old Virginia before the War.* New York, 1897.

Porter, Mrs. M. E. *Mrs. Porter's New Southern Cookery Book, and Companion for Frugal and Economical Housekeepers.* Philadelphia, 1871.

Randolph, Mary. *The Virginia Housewife: or, Methodical Cook.* Washington, 1831.

Reniers, Perceval. *The Springs of Virginia: Life, Love, and Death at the Waters, 1775-1900.* Chapel Hill, N.C., 1941.

Scott, Anne F. *The Southern Lady: From Pedestal to Politics, 1830-1930.* Chicago, 1970.

Sellers, John R. "The Leisure Time of the Plantation Mistress in Colonial Virginia." M.A. thesis, Tulane University, 1964.

Sontag, Susan. *Illness as Metaphor.* New York, 1979.

Sorley, Merrow E. *Lewis of Warner Hall.* Baltimore, 1979.

Spruill, Julia C. *Women's Life and Work in the Southern Colonies.* Chapel Hill, N.C., 1938.

Tannahill, Reay. *Food in History.* New York, 1973.

Tyree, Marion C. *Housekeeping in Old Virginia.* Louisville, 1879.

Ude, Louis. *The French Cook: A System of Fashionable and Economic Cookery Adapted to the Use of English Families.* Philadelphia, 1828.

Wertenbaker, Thomas J. *Patrician and Plebeian in Virginia.* New York, 1959.

Wilson, C. Anne. *Food and Drink in Britain.* New York, 1974.

Wilstach, Paul *Tidewater Virginia.* New York, 1929.

Woman's Day Encyclopedia of Cookery. 12 vols. New York, 1966.

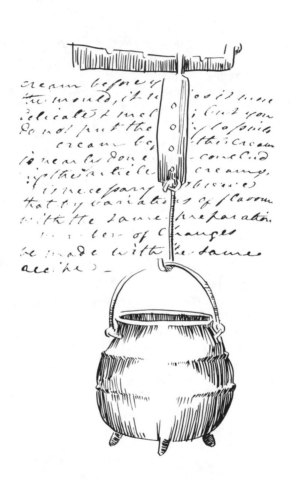

cream before putting in
the mould, it ___ ___ is more
delicate & mel____ ; but you
do not put the ___ ___ to ____
    cream be____ the cream
is nearly done ____ concluded
if the article ___ creamy,
is necessary ___ ___ there are
that by variations of flavour
with the same preparation
____ ___ ber of changes
be made with the same
article ___

Index

A Note on the Type

The body of this book is set on a Mergenthaler Linotron 202 in Bembo, a typeface originally cut in the fifteenth century by Francesco Griffo of Bologna, designer of the first Italic type. It first appears in Cardinal Bembo's *De Aetna* printed in 1495 by Aldus Manutius. Bembo greatly influenced Claude Garamond whose typeface designs set the European mode for two centuries. The contemporary version of Bembo was revived in 1929 by English Monotype.

Jacket design, book design and pen illustrations are by Michael Ledet of Ledet Mann Productions, New Orleans.

Typography, production, printing and binding are by A-R Editions, Inc., Madison, Wisconsin.

Pine apple cream

free the rind of a pine
apple in boiling cream, &
proceed as usual for other
rich — you must only
use the rind, for the pulp
being acid, the cream
would curdle. —

Jellies of fruit

is to be observed that all
jellies made of red fruit
must be worked cold, & be
put on ice very promptly
you use a thin mould
would alter the colour
spoil the taste; but if you
earthen moulds, the
jellies will always both
look & taste as they ought —
is also advisable to clarify